ROLAND ALLEN PIONEER, PRIEST, AND PROPHET

by his grandson
Hubert J.B. Allen

D0062231

Forward Movement Publications
Cincinnati, Ohio
Wm. B. Eerdmans Publishing Co.
Grand Rapids, Michigan

For the Eleven Great-Grandchildren

I sincerely hope that all those of my readers who agree with Sir Thomas Browne in the belief that 'there are in every man's life certain rubs, doublings, and wrenches, which pass a while under the effects of chance, but at last, well examined, prove the mere hand of God,' *will read in every page such striking proofs of the watchful care of God over His world as to stir them to high praise for His goodness, and to stronger and deeper faith in His all-wise government.*

The Siege of the Peking Legations, pp.viii-ix

Hubert John Brooke Allen was born in 1931 in what is nowadays Tanzania. He has served in numerous countries, notably Uganda, Nigeria, the Dominican Republic, and Great Britain; and for more than a dozen years he was Director of Training for the International Union of Local Authorities [IULA], based at The Hague, in Holland. Now an international consultant on training for municipal administration, he lives on the outskirts of Oxford with his Irish wife, Phoebe (a teacher); their three graduate children are also based in Oxford whenever they are in England.

Published by
Forward Movement Publications, 412 Sycamore St.,
Cincinnati,
OH 45202 USA
and by
Wm. B. Eerdmans Publishing Co.,
255 Jefferson Ave. SE, Grand Rapids, Michigan 49503 USA

Library of Congress Cataloging-in-Publication Data

Allen, Hubert J. B.
    Roland Allen : pioneer, priest, and prophet / by Hubert J. B. Allen.
        p.   cm.
    Includes bibliographical references and index.
    ISBN 0-8028-0897-2 (pbk. : alk. paper)
    1. Allen, Roland, 1869-1947. 2. Church of
England—Clergy—Biography. 3. Anglican
Communion—England—Clergy—Biography.
4. Missionaries—England—Biography. I. Title.
BX5199.A545A44 1995
266.'3'092—dc20
    [B]   95-18850
                                            CIP

Contents

Introduction and Acknowledgements .... *vii*

Foreword .... *xiii*

Prologue *1*

1: Family Background and Early Years *9*

2: First Years in China *21*

3: The Gathering Storm *33*

4: The Siege of the Peking Legations.1 .... *43*

5: Furlough; and Engagement *55*

6: Marriage and Yung-Ch'ing *67*

7: The End of the Beginning *77*

8: The World Dominion Movement and World War I *91*

9: Peace and Beaconsfield *105*

10: Non-Professional Missionaries *117*

11: Travelling Salesman *129*

12: The Case for Voluntary Clergy *141*

13: East Africa *151*

14: Faithful Soldier and Servant *161*

Epilogue *171*

Appendix 1: Some Relationships Mentioned in the Text *177*

Appendix 2: The resignation letter *183*

Appendix 3: Advice to an active voluntary
   clergyman in the Sudan *189*

Appendix 4: Letter to all Bishops attending
   1930 Lambeth Conference *195*

Appendix 5: Missionary Methods: St. Paul's or Satan's? *197*

Appendix 6: Letter withdrawing assistance from
   St. Mark's Church, Nairobi *215*

References: Books and Pamphlets by and about Roland Allen *217*

Index *223*

Introduction and Acknowledgements

During his lifetime my grandfather, Roland Allen, was not very widely known. So I was more than a little startled, when introduced to a Bishop in the early 1960s, to be swept into a warm episcopal embrace, accompanied by the remark: *I hear you are the Grandson of the Prophet!*

As I mention later in this biographical note, I can recall, when I was about twelve years old, asking my 'Granfer' whether I could read his books, and receiving from him the reply: *Oh, yes, you can read them by all means—but you won't understand them; I don't think anyone is going to understand them until I've been dead ten years . . .*

He died in 1947, so he was perhaps a little too pessimistic: for not very long afterwards some of these books were finding at least one enthusiastic and influential reader in the person of my friendly Bishop—Lesslie Newbigin of the Church of South India, who was then Director of the Division of World Mission and Evangelism of the World Council of Churches. As early as 1952, at the joint conference of the WCC and the International Missionary Council at Willingen in Germany, Dr. Newbigin was beginning to urge people to seek out Granfer's books; as he later remarked in the preface to a new edition of Roland's most renowned book, once someone *has started reading Allen, he will be compelled to go on. He will find that this quiet voice has a strange relevance and immediacy for the problems of the church in our day.*[1] I

---

[1]Foreword to the American edition of *Missionary Methods: St.Paul's or Ours?* (Eerdmans, Grand Rapids—1962, *reprinted 1993*)

am honoured and delighted that Bishop Newbigin has consented to add a discerning Foreword to this memoir.

From the time of the Willingen meeting onwards, Granfer's writings began to become more and more influential, to such an extent that in certain circles he has nowadays almost been transformed into a cult figure.

One consequence of this growing interest has been that numerous scholars have written studies about Roland Allen and his ideas; and to several of these studies have been appended biographical notes, one or two of which have been sent to members of his family for comment. Whilst almost all of them have been well-intentioned and fairly accurate, many of them have portrayed a rather dry theologian, rather than a warm and kindly—if rather austere and argumentative—human being: *adept at giving the opposite viewpoint to a speaker, merely to get things going!*[2]

In an effort to bring his personality a little bit more to life, therefore, I have ventured to assemble the material in the ensuing memoir. Granfer himself would have been most unlikely to approve of any such endeavour, for his Tractarian background had inculcated in him a horror of any sort of 'cult of personality'. As David Paton points out, Granfer (in his study of S.J.W. Clark, his colleague and sponsor) exhibits his disdain for this chatty and intimate type of biography.[3]

In his introduction to a series of articles about a tour of Canada, during which he *travelled to the Pacific and back by different routes to see what a visitor could see of the real state of the Church there*, Roland dashes the biographer's hopes with the remark: *I do not propose to describe my journey, still less the people whom I met.* Similarly, in a characteristic letter from Assam he remarks to his son:

---

[2]See Chapter XIV below.

[3]See McLeish in D.M. Paton, *Reform of the Ministry* (World Dominion Press, 1960), p.14.

*I am not sending any diary this week. I had an interesting &
pleasing ride on an elephant into the jungle & a view of
another tea-garden in the making, but that is not the sort of
stuff that I want to put in a diary.*[4]

Likewise he would always try his best to escape being
photographed or, if civility made that difficult to avoid, to make
himself as inconspicuous as possible on the very edge of whatever wedding or baptismal group he might find himself involved in. Most of the photographs we possess were taken for
obligatory purposes, as official portraits for his parish or society,
or for the furtherance of their work. Often, too, he was himself
the photographer, so he is safely out of the picture.

If I need an excuse for my reprehensible inquisitiveness,
however, it is provided in Granfer's own words, when he
remarks: *Alter, even a little, some element in my birth and upbringing, and I might be taking a very different view.*[5] If we are to
understand the prophet, perhaps it may help us to know about
these things.

Additional problems for me have arisen because our 'Grannie' (Roland's wife, Beatrice) was tremendously protective, so
that if any of we three grandchildren began to ask him questions
she was almost certain to intervene, to tell us to run along and
not tire him. Moreover, his children—my father and my Aunt
Priscilla—surprisingly seldom spoke to us of their parents or of
their own childhood. Partly this was because our *mother* was
always ready to delve for us in her own almost inexhaustible
treasure-chest of memories of a truly fascinating childhood and
later life—under Porfirio Diaz, and during the Mexican Revolution, in France during the First World War, at Oxford University
and the Sorbonne in the 'twenties, and in colonial East Africa
during the 'thirties and the Second World War: so as children we
were fully supplied with entrancing reminiscences, and did not

---

[4]Letter to Iohn (in the Sudan), 18 November 1927.
[5]See 'The Family Rite' in *Reform of the Ministry, op. cit.,* p. 200.

seek to probe the Allen family memories until it was too late . . .

Some of what follows is based on boxes of family memorabilia preserved by Grannie, which came to light only recently, after my wife and I took over my parents' home in Marston Village, near Oxford; and on Granfer's own papers on deposit in the helpful care of the library staff of Rhodes House, across the river in Oxford itself.[6] In addition I have had help from my two sisters and from several other members of Roland's family (in particular from his nephew Derick—F. W. Allen—and from his wife's niece, Finetta Chamberlain (née Brandreth); from various friends (notably Mr. Martin Holmes, FSA; Mrs. Barbara Saben, CBE; and Miss Valerie Fliess); and from some of the many scholars and theologians, who have written about Granfer's work (e.g. the Revd. John T. Pilling, the Revd. Canon H. Boone Porter, and the Revd. Åke Talltorp). To all of these I am truly grateful, not least for the books and documents they have provided or which they have arranged for others, such as the Archivist of the Anglican Church of Canada, to send to me.

My sketch of Granfer's early life has been consolidated and confirmed in particular from two sources: firstly, unpublished notes about the life and background of Roland's elder brother, Willoughby Charles Allen, which were compiled by his son, the late Brigadier R.M. (Dick) Allen; and, secondly, painstaking and scrupulous investigations by Captain David Sanderson (Church Army) during the preparation of his Lambeth Diploma thesis, *Roland Allen and his Vision of the Spontaneous Expansion of the Church*. I should like to express especial gratitude for being allowed to garner the fruits of those researches.

Most of the photographs were found in Grannie's boxes, or have been lent to me for copying by Cousin Derick. The plans of

---

[6]After Roland's death all but a few private papers were handed over to the Survey Application Trust, and at a later date to USPG (the United Society for the Propagation of the Gospel); that Society has now entrusted them to the Bodleian Library at Oxford, which keeps them in its Rhodes House branch. Several of the Appendices to this memoir are among those documents.

Peking are from Granfer's own published account of the siege of the legations. The drawing of the church at Chalfont St. Peter is reproduced by kind permission of the present Rector and churchwardens.

There is only myself to blame for any ineptitudes in the use of the word-processor. I have to thank my sons and daughter for their encouragement, and my wife for her patience, when its idiosyncracies have impaired my temper.

Hubert J.B. Allen
Marston Village, Oxford—1994

Foreword

Roland Allen was, in his time, a lonely prophet. His ideas seemed to most of his contemporaries eccentric and unrealistic. I retain vivid memories of my own reading of Allen's work, when I was beginning missionary service in India. I fought against his ideas—but it was a losing battle. His writing had a kind of bulldog grip, and you could not shake them off. Today many of the things for which he argued are generally accepted: that ordination to the priesthood is not identical with induction into a salaried profession; that Christian disunity is a scandal and an absurdity; that the Eucharist is the essential centre of the life of the Church; and (of course) that the churches of the former 'mission fields' ought to be entirely free of dependence on the missionary agencies which officiated at their birth. These ideas, radical when Allen canvassed them, are now commonplace. Do we still have anything to learn from this pioneer and prophet? I think so.

At the centre of Allen's message was the conviction that the Holy Spirit is the active agent in the Christian mission. For him Pentecost was the key for the understanding of mission. He could write about 'The Spontaneous Expansion of the Church' because he saw it, not as a human enterprise, but as a divine activity. To understand that, is to be delivered from the anxieties, the burdens and the sense of guilt which so often form the atmosphere of discussion about mission. Missionary thinking is still pervaded by Pelagianism. Mission is conceived as a task, rather than as a gift, an over-spill, and an explosion of joy. Allen's insistence that mission is not one of the tasks of the Church, but rather the very being of the Church itself, is misunderstood if the experience of the presence and power of the Holy Spirit is not constitutive of churchmanship. In his formative years as a missionary in China, Allen was learning to prise the missionary calling loose from its colonial moorings; to see what he was engaged in, not as Christendom extending its power, but as a fresh and always surprising work of the living Spirit of God. As churches of the old Christendom try to come to terms with the progressive paganization of the 'Western' world, they have not yet learned what Allen had to teach about mission, as an always fresh and surprising work of the Spirit.

But Allen was not a prototype of the contemporary evangelical charismatic—much as I think he would have welcomed the charismatic explosion. He was a priest in the Catholic tradition of the Church of England. His spiritual home was in Oxford's Pusey House. He had a firm conviction of the reality, the given-ness and the power of the gospel, the sacraments, and the apostolic ministry. His central conviction that mission is the work of the Holy Spirit was integrally bound up with, and not detached from, this confidence in the reality and power of these given realities. Those who first joined him in disseminating his ideas (through the Survey Application Trust) were of a different churchmanship, with the result that this essential Catholic ingredient in Allen's missiology has often been forgotten. Those who tried to put Allen's principles into practice have generally been Evangelical Protestants. It is only much more recently that Roman Catholics like Leonardo Boff and Vincent Donovan have, without any preceding contact with Allen's work, struck out in the same direction.

Because I believe in the continuing importance of Allen's ideas, I am very glad that we now have a full-length account of him which sets his teaching in the context of his whole life and character. I hope this will lead to a fresh discovery of his ideas, and I think this could be fruitful in at least two respects.

Firstly in respect of the mission of the local congregation in the very discouraging mission fields of pagan Europe and North America. In England, certainly, a strong dose of Roland Allen's missiology would have a wonderful effect in loosening up the stiff joints and muscles of the typical congregation, of whatever denomination, and would bring a liberating confidence in the power of the Holy Spirit to bring his own witness into the life of the world.

Secondly I think that Allen's ideas are significant for the present moment in the development of the ecumenical movement. During the past century this movement has been concerned with the relationships between the main Christian confessions as they are organized locally, nationally and globally. But we seem now to be in a situation where the growing edges of the Church are not in these bodies but in the increasing numbers of independent bodies of Christians: house churches, 'independent Christian fellowships', 'base communities' and so on. It seems to be in such movements as these that the signs of vitality are evident. In one respect they reflect Allen's central teaching about the role of the Holy Spirit in the life and growth of the Church. They generally lack, however, the other element of his teaching—the objectivity, given-ness and power of sacraments and the apostolic ministry linking them to the universal Church. Many in these movements seek to escape from the rigidities of the old 'Christendom' patterns, but do not see, as Allen did, that one can cherish the elements of order which give coherence to the universal Church and yet be free from the heavy structures with which these elements have been associated during the centuries of 'Christendom.' It seems to me that it is in this direction that the movement for Christian unity must move in the immediately coming decades, and I think that the missiology of Roland Allen could powerfully contribute to such a development.

Lesslie Newbigin
Herne Hill, May 1994

The Rt. Revd. Dr. J.E. Lesslie Newbigin, CBE, theologian, author and preacher, was for many years a missionary in India, and became one of the first Bishops of the ecumenical Church of South India, inaugurated in 1947. For a period he was Director of the Division of World Mission and Evangelism at the World Council of Churches.

Prologue

Roland Allen has been called a 20th century prophet. In the many years since his death international conferences have been held and articles have been published to discuss his ideas in Hawaii and in India, in Germany and Japan, in Santo Domingo and Washington, D.C. He has been described by a Presbyterian as *a faithful disciple of the Anglican tradition with a leaning towards the Catholic content;*[1] yet *Allen's vision embraces Evangelical, Catholic, Liberal and what we now call 'Charismatic' elements;*[2] *his use of Scripture and methodology seem to align him with the liberation theologians of today*.[3]

Moreover, his writings have been an inspiration for Pentecostals and for Jesuits, for Lutherans and Baptists, for scholars writing in Japanese and in German, in Swedish and in Dutch, in Spanish and in Afrikaans, at least as much as for his fellow Anglicans in many parts of the world. One writer describes him as the prophet of the *independent and self-governing Younger Churches;*[4] for another he is *sometimes referred to as the prophet of NSM* (the non-stipendiary ministry).[5]

But who—or what—*is* 'a prophet'?

Perhaps it would be a fair definition to describe a prophet as a person, who has the perspicacity to observe truths that are

---

[1]Alexander McLeish, a Church of Scotland minister: see D. M. Paton, *The Ministry of the Spirit* (World Dominion Press, 1960), p. xii.

[2]David Sanderson, 'Roland Allen: a Prophet for a "Decade of Evangelism",' *Quarterly of the Modern Churchpeople's Union*, XXXIV (1993), p. 14.

[3]Alan Hargrave, *But Who Will Preside?* (Nottingham: Grove Books, 1990), p. 14.

[4]Stephen Neill, *Colonialism & Christian Missions* (Lutterworth, 1966), p. 418.

[5]Patrick Vaughan, in J. Fuller and P. Vaughan, *Working for the Kingdom* (SPCK, 1986), p. 171.

unfashionable, and the tactlessness to voice them. In this way the prophet greatly annoys whoever those people are that happen to be the contemporary 'pillars of society': because the prophet makes them feel uncomfortable, and rather less confident of their own wisdom and their own worth.

Like many prophets before him, Roland was conscious of the enormity of his proposals and his accusations, and often riddled with self-doubt: *I have never in my life been able to convince myself that I did any act from one pure motive. I might think at the time that I did, but it would not bear examination.* Nevertheless, like many such prophets: *I was compelled to do it. I could not escape.*[6]

Another characteristic of true prophets, from Isaiah and Galileo to Darwin and Einstein, has been the phenomenon that some time later—often quite abruptly—those same truths, that were first so tactlessly pointed out by the prophet, come to be almost universally accepted, so that it is quite difficult to understand what all the fuss was about. What Roland wrote of his colleague, Sidney Clark, can be applied with even more force to himself:

> *the truth which he enunciated must be supreme. Not until it has so much become the truth of others that they scarcely know whence they got it, and if asked, can hardly recall its source, has he really succeeded. When men say of a truth which he laboriously hammered out, that it is common knowledge, a truth which anyone knows, or can see for himself, without any teaching, or when they express it as if they had known it for ages, or had thought it out for themselves, then and not till then, has a man like Clark really done his work.*[7]

So it has been with Roland Allen. Fundamental to his ideas was one single concept: what one commentator has called *the*

---

[6]See Note 10 below.

[7]*Sidney James Wells Clark—a Vision of Foreign Missions* (World Dominion Press, 1937), pp. 166-67.

high and lofty significance which Allen ascribed to the Holy Spirit.[8] This—which has been seen as premonitory of the Charismatic Movement[9]—led to several consequences in his life.

He started his career as a Christian missionary: but after a while he began to bring into question the accepted practices of most missionaries of his day. Those missionaries, he observed, sought to convey with them, and to perpetuate overseas, the orthodoxies of their homelands, with all the trappings and accretions, and particularly the competing sects that reflect many centuries of Western church history. *The difficulty today,* he complained, *is that Christians acknowledge that others have the Spirit, and yet do not recognize that they ought to be, and must be, because spiritually they are, in communion with one another.*[10]

The proper role of missionaries, Roland propounded, was not to do these things; but on the contrary to do no more than St. Paul had sought to do. That is to say, to convey to heathen peoples the basic elements of Christianity—the 'signs of the Kingdom': namely the Bible, the Creed, the Ministry, and the Sacraments. Thereafter, like St. Paul, suggested Roland, the missionaries should exhibit sufficient faith confidently to entrust the future of the Church to the Holy Spirit: for He would know infinitely better than any foreign intruders how to work out God's purposes in and through the local people, making full use of all their special talents and unique insights.

Next Roland became the vicar of a typical English country parish: and once again he soon began to question accepted practice. The Church of England—the established church of the nation—required clergy to provide Sacraments even to *men and women who openly deny the truth of the Creeds or by the immorality of their lives openly defy the laws of God.*

---

[8]Harry R. Boer, *Pentecost & Missions* (Grand Rapids: Wm. B. Eerdmans, 1961), p. 299.

[9]See e.g. John E. Brammer, "Roland Allen: Pioneer in a Spirit-Centred Theology of Mission," *Missiology,* V/2 (April 1977), p. 175.

[10]*Pentecost & the World* (London: Oxford University Press, 1917), p. 86.

Although this was the law of the land, Roland was puzzled that *a great many good and thoughtful men* were prepared to tolerate this state of affairs. He himself felt so strongly that he could not conscientiously do so that he decided to resign, even though he knew the consequence: *I cannot act as I am determined to act, and yet hold any benefice in England.*[11]

Thus constrained to become a voluntary clergyman, and a freelance writer, Roland went on to question accepted practice even further: *You will think, my Lord,* he wrote to one bishop, *that I have nothing else to do but to ask questions. It is not far off the truth. I desire to give my whole time and strength to these questions; it is by examining our commonplace assertions that I hope we may find some truth.*[12]

What he now did was to draw attention to the failure of the Anglican Church to make adequate provision of the 'signs of the Kingdom' even for its own flock. As a Swedish Lutheran notes:

> *Roland Allen in his writings clearly and frequently emphasizes the necessity of the sacramental life . . . This sacramental dimension was to him a matter of course, and a condition necessary for the growth and expansion of the Church in mission.*[13]

In the Catechism of the Book of Common Prayer it is stated categorically that the Sacrament of *the Supper of the Lord* is *generally necessary to salvation.* By insistence on prolonged, very specialised academic training and qualifications for a full-time professional clergy, Roland pointed out, the Church was finding itself unable to extend to all its people the regular and frequent access to Sacraments that its own doctrines proclaimed to be 'necessary to salvation'.

The solution to this, he suggested, as with missionary methods, was to return to the practice of the early Church:

---

[11]See Appendix 2.

[12]Letter to the Bishop of Kampala, 24 October 1927.

[13]Åke Talltorp, *Sacrament & Growth* (Uppsala, Sweden: 1989), p. 67.

namely, for the Bishop to seek out and ordain people possessing no more than the qualifications demanded by the writer of the First Epistle to Timothy 3:2-9. Among the fifteen specified, observes Roland, *There is not one purely literary or intellectual qualification demanded; there is not a hint that any question of salary was in the Apostle's mind.*[14] These 'voluntary clergy',[15] earning their living by any legitimate means, would be available in every parish, not merely to assist and supplement the stipendiary clergy, but to provide the people of God with uninterrupted access to the Church's Sacraments.

Roland believed—on the basis of e.g. 1 Peter 4:10—that *there is a priesthood which belongs inherently to all Christians,*[16] so that, in his view, a single Christian, or a group of Christians, isolated for any unavoidable reason from the rest of the Church, could exercise the priestly office, and administer and partake of the Sacraments. In the Eucharist, after all, Christ is the Priest; and where two or three are gathered in His Name, He is there in the midst of them. Where He is, there is the Priest.[17]

Nevertheless, this could apply only in exceptional circumstances; as soon as possible a fit and proper person should be ordained priest, to administer the Sacraments within the community. But such a 'fit and proper person' did not necessarily need to have professional academic training; it was quite enough for him to have the guidance and direction of the Holy Spirit. *Christ ordained His Sacraments for His people without any proviso that they must not meet to observe His commands unless they have a paid professional to minister to them.*

---

[14]*The Canadian Churchman,* 26 June, 1924.

[15]Not 'part-time priests': *A cleric can no more be a half-time cleric than a father can be a half-time father, or a baptized Christian a half-time Christian,* expostulates Roland in *The Case for Voluntary Clergy* (London: Eyre & Spottiswoode, 1930), p. 89.

[16]See *Appendix 3B,* postscript.

[17]See 'The Priesthood of the Church,' *Church Quarterly Review* (January 1933), pp. 233-244.

In placing the eucharistic sacrament at the centre of church life, Roland was anticipating by many years the central teaching of the Liturgical Movement within Anglican Churches. Today the revised prayer books and the custom of Anglican churches in most parts of the world provide the Eucharist as the chief and normal service every Sunday. In Roland's day even large and well attended parish churches, with a full complement of clergy, were accustomed to weekly Mattins and Evensong, with a Communion Service no more than once a month.

The Ecumenical Movement was another transformation of ecclesiastical attitudes anticipated by Roland long before significant changes began to take place:

> If the Holy Ghost is given, those to whom He is given are certainly accepted in Christ by God . . . Men may separate them, systems may part them from the enjoyment and strength of their unity; but, if they share the one Spirit, they are one.
>
> Men who hold a theory of the Church which excludes from communion those whom they admit to have the Spirit of Christ simply proclaim that their theory is in flat contradiction to the spiritual fact.[18]

Nowadays none of these ideas is particularly startling: indeed they are in the mainstream of theological understanding, and it is quite hard to believe that Roland Allen could have been looked upon as an isolated and irrelevant eccentric. The full handover of missionary churches to indigenous Christians is accepted practice; clergy hesitate to dispense sacraments as if they were merely social niceties; the Eucharist is the normal Sunday service; ecumenical approaches are commonplace; and the ordination of Anglican priests in the 'non-stipendiary ministry' is an increasingly familiar, if relatively timid, move towards Roland's conception of 'voluntary clergy'.

But Roland's prophetic utterances did not cease, even when

---

[18]*Pentecost & the World, op. cit.,* pp. 85, 86.

he became an old man. When we have reviewed his life, we should return to consider whether those, or his more accepted ideas, can have any continuing significance, even as late as the closing decade of the twentieth century.

CHAPTER I

Family Background and Early Years

'a very determined, not to say obstinate, person'
Priscilla Allen (née Malpas), c. 1890

Where, then, did this prophet come from?

There does not seem to be anything very remarkable about his forebears. The Allens were traditionally respectable Nottinghamshire stocking manufacturers. The family firm, founded during the 18th century, records supplying at least one pair of stockings to Queen Victoria. It traded—until a takeover in fairly recent years—as Allen, Solly & Company. The last member of the Allen family to be associated with this firm was a certain Lionel Raymond Allen (the son of Roland's first cousin), who died in 1984, shortly after his 100th birthday.[1]

Roland's grandfather, James Roger Allen (1793-1872), served as Chamberlain and Senior Councillor and later as an Alderman of Nottingham city; whilst his great-grandfather, John Allen (1754-1832), was the Sheriff of Nottingham, in 1795 and 1801. Roland's father, Charles Fletcher Allen (1835-1873), was James Roger's second son: he graduated from Christ's College, Cambridge in 1858, and became a clergyman in the Church of England, as did all his own three surviving sons.

Charles Fletcher started work as a curate in Gloucestershire, where in 1862 he married one of the many daughters of his first vicar. A couple of years later he went to Derby as both curate of Radbourne and a teacher of mathematics, and—at an early age—headmaster of St. Clement's School. He was also something of a scholar, being the author and translator of an edition of writings of St. Chrysostom.[2]

Roland (Granfer) was born on 29th December 1868 at 104, Friargate. The family lived in Uttoxeter New Road; Roland was the sixth of Charles Fletcher's seven children. He was baptized in St. Werburgh's Church some four weeks later.

Not long afterwards, my great-grandfather's career went abruptly into decline. He left his headmastership in Derby, firstly to hold a brief curacy at Handsworth in Birmingham, where he took services in July and August 1871; less than a year later he was officiating at Enmore Green in Dorset. And shortly after that, he travelled out to the colony of British Honduras, without his family. During one week of 1873, in October, records show that he conducted several services in St. John's Anglican Church in Belize; but only a week later he died there, at the early age of thirty-eight—that is to say, when Roland was still less than five years old.[3]

---

[1] Information supplied to David Sanderson by Mr Geoffrey Oldfield of the Nottingham Family History Society.

[2] *Four Discources of Chrysostom. Chiefly on the Parables of the Rich Man and Lazarus* (Longmans, 1869) [author's name given simply as 'F.Allen'].

[3] See David Sanderson, 'Roland Allen and his Vision', Lambeth Diploma thesis, 1989, and Talltorp, *op. cit.*

The charitable story is that Charles Fletcher felt an abrupt 'call' to drop everything, in order to go off to work for a missionary society; and that he died of yellow fever very soon after he was appointed. But in fact no records exist to show that he joined or was sent by any of the British societies then active in Central America. It is perhaps possible that he was directly invited by the local British community to come to Belize as their chaplain; but it seems odd, to say the least, that his pious widow should in that case never have alluded to such a martyr's death.

The very swift and sudden death itself may well have been a consequence of yellow fever. Nevertheless, suggestions that the deterioration in his fortunes was in fact caused by *delirium tremens*, resulting from chronic alcoholism, may be equally well founded: for such a very sudden reversal certainly seems to indicate some scandal. So does the fact that none of the other members of his own affluent (but irreproachably respectable) Allen family appear to have done anything at all to help his poor widow, who went with her numerous children to live with her parents; significantly, perhaps, neither she nor her maid, Hannah, ever spoke to her children or grandchildren about their Allen relatives.[4]

Roland himself was abstemious, but never a total abstainer. He used to drink Australian Burgundy as a tonic, and advised a nephew to do the same. In the 1940s in Nairobi he would often partake of a small glass of sherry before dinner, if there were visitors. His children both used to enjoy the traditional East African 'sun-downer', but they, too, seldom drank more than a couple of glasses of anything alcoholic, and this may have been partly because their father seems to have warned them about 'a family tendency' towards drink and drugs—even though none of their relations can recall any other examples of this.

---

[4]Some of those wealthy stocking manufacturers, however, seem to have had a continuing interest in their poor relations. Soon after Roland joined the Mission in North China, its accounts begin to record generous contributions from 'J.R. Allen, Esq' and 'R. Allen, Esq', both of Nottingham.

Roland, then, never really knew his father. What is more, his grandparents also died before he was ten years old, so his mother alone became the principal formative influence on the young boy. This widow of Charles Fletcher Allen had been born Priscilla Malpas. Her father, Joseph Henry Malpas (1788-1877) was reputedly a rather sombre, humourless man. For no less than fifty years he was vicar of Awre, on the north bank of the Severn in Gloucestershire; he married twice, and had nineteen children, fifteen of them girls. It is said that at one time the young men of Bristol used to turn out on Sunday mornings to watch the Miss Malpases going to church, two and two, in a long procession. All of them were alleged to have been very plain; but almost all of them got married—at least three of them to clergymen.

Priscilla's parents died within a few years of Charles Fletcher's death in Honduras, so she was left on her own. Nevertheless, she succeeded in raising six of her seven children to adulthood, with the help of her utterly devoted servant, Hannah Clissold. Hannah was a Somersetshire woman, who entered Priscilla's service as a nurse girl, when she was only about fourteen years old. When her services were no longer strictly necessary, Priscilla found her a job with a wealthier family: but Hannah soon pleaded to be taken back, on even less than the pitifully small wage of an adult maidservant in Victorian days.

Priscilla was of a strongly evangelical persuasion; some of her relatives were Plymouth Brethren, including her younger sister, Catherine Emma—*a timid, sweet-natured little woman who . . . acted for them as a 'colporteur', patrolling the park in search of tramps to whom she would give one of the little 'tracts' which she always carried in her bag*. Priscilla herself was not of the Brethren, but she was a very determined, not to say obstinate, person (characteristics which Roland seems to have inherited). She had little patience with 'free thinkers'. One of her grandsons recalled asking her to explain some apparently irreconcilable statements

12

in the Bible and being told firmly: *You see, Dear, there are some things which it is not given to us to understand.*

Understanding was one thing; ignorance was another. During the last months of her life, she had an interview with an insurance agent or some such person. Afterwards she remarked that he was a singularly ill-informed young man: *Do you know,* she grumbled, *he had never even heard of Ehud!* Those of her family, who were acquainted with the obscure story in the Book of Judges about this sanguinary left-hander,[5] could only speculate why these two persons' conversation should have included any allusion to the son of Gera the Benjamite.

But another of the grandchildren was deeply impressed by another aspect of her character:

Serenity is the authentic mark of the old evangelical: exemplified for me, unforgettably, by my own grandmother, born in 1839, who carried right on into the thirties of this century the tradition of the old Evangelical Movement. Her serenity I never saw disturbed, and her praying—almost always, even when alone, vocal—was the completely natural communion of her soul with the in-dwelling Christ. I remember as a boy of 9 or 10 passing her door one night on my way upstairs to bed, and hearing her talking, so I thought at first, to some companion in her room: but the companion, I soon found out, was Christ; and there was no difference that I could mark in the style and manner of her talking to Him from the quiet, dignified, gentle tone which she used to everyone else. She passed from one to the other with the utmost simplicity and without effort—so slight was the barrier between the two worlds: in both she was at home, and altogether herself.[6]

---

[5] Judges 3:15-30.

[6] This account by Roland's nephew, Peter, with much following information, is contained in unpublished notes on the Allen family written by Peter's brother, Dick (Brigadier R.M.Allen, 2nd son of Willoughby).

It is more than likely that Roland is alluding to his mother's influence when he remarks that: *In the days of my childhood I used often to hear people talk of something which they called 'experimental religion'. They meant, I fancy, religion based upon a personal experience . . . of the reality of such great doctrines as the forgiveness of sins, of the grace of Christ's presence, of the indwelling of the Holy Ghost . . . I believe that this teaching of experimental religion is profoundly true. Religious knowledge . . . cannot be attained by mere repetition of religious creeds, and such like.*[7]

It was from Priscilla, too, that Roland learnt, as he was many years later to remark to his son, that: *in the Church there is a point at which rebellion is justifiable for the good of the Church, not for any personal end.* In his long and frank correspondence with the Bishop of Assam he challenges Hubback's submissive obedience to his Metropolitan with the remark:

> *My mother was certainly right when she taught me that to speak of oneself as obeying the Church, and to speak of oneself as obeying Christ are not identical. It makes a great difference to our life whether we think habitually in terms of Christ or any other than Christ, whether we habitually say Christ gave me this work to do, or someone else gave it to me to do, and it affects others to whom we speak.*[8]

I myself can *just* remember Priscilla and Hannah from a visit in about 1935. My 'Great-Grannie' was then in her mid-nineties, bedridden in a comfortable home provided by her children in north Oxford's Norham Road. She wished to give her great-grandson a book, so my parents went into town and selected one of Beatrix Potter's stories for me. However, Great-Grannie insisted on keeping it to read to herself overnight: it was a rule of hers, she explained, never to give to anyone a book she had

---

[7]*Educational Principles & Missionary Methods* (London: Robert Scott, 1919), p. 103.

[8]Letter of March 1st, 1928: reprinted in Paton, *Reform of the Ministry, op. cit.*, p.153.

not read herself. Happily, *The Tale of Samuel Whiskers* met with her approval.

In the 1880s Priscilla Allen had practically no money: allegedly Charles Fletcher had failed to pay his last life assurance premium before he left for Honduras, so the policy was nullified. Consequently all four surviving sons had to win scholarships in order to get themselves through school and university. Whilst still an undergraduate at Oxford, one of the four (Arthur) fell through the ice, when he was skating on the River Cherwell: his body was later recovered, far downstream. The other three boys—Reginald, Willoughby and Roland himself—all went on after graduation to take Holy Orders in the Church of England.

To digress briefly, it may be of interest to summarize the careers of Roland's surviving sister and brothers. (Another sister, 'Nellie'—Ellen Ida—was a chronic invalid, who died of a fall at Paignton at the age of 33.)

Katy (Catherine Mary), like the Brontë sisters, was sent to the Clergy Daughters' School, and emulated the fictional 'Jane Eyre' by first earning herself a living as paid companion to the daughter of a wealthy businessman (a certain Bartholomew Jones, a widower living in Vienna), and by then going on to marry her employer. In Vienna she moved in relatively high society (she recalled, for example, meeting King Ludwig's paramour, Lola Montez); and when her husband died ten years' later he left her quite well provided for. 'Aunt Katy' was a great support to her mother in her old age, and always a generous friend to her nephews and nieces.

Reginald graduated from Sidney Sussex College, Cambridge. Except for his curacy, and the duration of the First World War, both of which periods were spent in the Gloucestershire parish of Blakeney, he spent most of his life abroad. For a time he was a chaplain in Darmstadt, where a music student in about 1890 used to recall being rebuked by him for attending the opera on Sundays. Later for nineteen years he was chaplain of a school for European boys at Bournabat, near Smyrna in Turkey; and a few years after the war he settled down as the chaplain to the British community at Dinan, near St. Malo in Brittany.

Willoughby Charles was much the most distinguished of the brothers during his lifetime. After starting in Cambridge as a pupil teacher at Fitzwilliam House, he heard that Oxford's Exeter College offered the Hasker Scholarship, to be won through an examination in Hebrew. He therefore taught himself Hebrew, *walked* from Cambridge to Oxford, and won the scholarship! Subsequently he was to win several other awards and prizes,[9] graduating with first class honours in theology and in oriental studies. He was ordained in 1894 to a curacy in South Hinksey, outside Oxford; and his college soon afterwards appointed him to be their Chaplain-Fellow. Later he became Sub-Rector of the college and Junior Proctor of the University.

From 1908 to 1916 Willoughby was both Archdeacon of Manchester and Principal of the Egerton Hall theological college. He then became simultaneously Rector of Chorley, Archdeacon of Blackburn, and an army chaplain. These exhausting combinations of duties aggravated a chronic ill health, originally occasioned by serious malnutrition during early years at the Clergy Orphan School in Canterbury. Charles Holmes (later Director of the National Gallery in London) used to recall how he and Willoughby at times became so desperate that they would go out and steal turnips to augment their meagre diet. This ill-health dogged Willoughby throughout the rest of his working life as a parish priest in Lancashire and in Norfolk, and after his retirement; nevertheless he outlived all his brothers and sisters, not dying until 1953.

Notwithstanding his poor health, he long continued his scholarly work. Perhaps his most influential study was his *Critical and Exegetical Commentary on the Gospel of St. Matthew*, which was published in the International Critical Commentary in 1908, the year he left Oxford for Manchester; later on he wrote

---

[9]The Pusey & Ellerton scholarship, the Kennicot scholarship, and the Houghton Prize for Syriac.

some much briefer commentaries, one on St. Mark's Gospel, and an *Introduction to the Books of the New Testament*. He also published a collection of his own sermons and addresses, which he called *The Christian Hope*. He gave the address at Roland's and Beatrice's wedding in 1901; and 'Uncle Willie' was to become the favourite uncle of their two children.

Interestingly, there do not appear to be any records or memories of theological debates between the learned Willoughby and his brilliant, but much less orthodox, younger brother. It may be speculated that they knew their views to be incompatible, and consequently preferred to avoid dissension. However, it may be no coincidence that another scholar at Exeter College was Professor W. M. Ramsay, whose writings on the early Church, and on St. Paul's travels, were to be of seminal importance for Roland later on, when he came to write Missionary Methods.[10]

To return to that younger brother, Roland: before he too went up to Oxford, he attended first Bath College school, and then, from 1884 to 1887, the Bristol Grammar School, where he was in the Classical VI.[11] He was a notably active member of the school's Debating Society, in years when it was dominated by T.R. Glover. It is characteristic that, in a debate between *Total Abstinence* and *Temperance,* Roland spoke in favour of temperance—the winning side. In other debates he voted in favour of motions that *Free Schools would be for the advantage of the nation*, and that *Horse-racing is pernicious.* In a motion moved by Glover— that *Thackeray was a better writer than Dickens*—Roland supported Dickens (who won, 20-10). He is also recorded as speaking in a debate between *Free Trade and "Fair Trade"*; and, as an Old Boy, returned to move—successfully—that *Britain's national defences are inadequate.*

---

[10]See Chapter VII below.

[11]Information supplied to David Sanderson by the Brtistol Grammar School's Archivist through Dr. John McKay.

17

He also played for the school at cricket, in the 1st XI; and he was on the cricket committee. He is described as *A fair left-handed bat, but very nervous on first going in; has not come off this year; fields well, and is a safe catch.*

In spite of this evidence of athletic prowess, it is nevertheless remarkable that he proved sufficiently healthy to win, not only a scholarship to St. John's College, Oxford (the Bristol Grammar School's closed Sir Thomas White Scholarship), but also, later on, the University's Lothian Prize, for a distinguished essay on Pope Silvester II, which was published in full in the learned journal, The English Historical Review.[12] He was also a founder member and secretary of the undergraduate theological study group, the Origen Society.[13]

These achievements seem remarkable, because during the whole of this time as an undergraduate (and throughout his life) he seemed to be suffering from a mysterious 'weak heart', which alarmed every doctor. All through his Oxford career his medical advisors would allow him to work for no more than one hour a day; and they forbade him to undertake any strenuous exercise. It is very possible that nowadays this 'murmur' would have given less cause for concern; but at that time it greatly worried the doctors, although a Wimpole Street specialist disapproved of the very strict regime imposed on him at Oxford, and encouraged him to take regular exercise, although to avoid sudden exertion.

In such circumstances Roland did well to achieve Second Class Honours—both in Classical Moderations in 1888, and in the Final School of History two years later. His *tutor and benefactor all the time I was at at St. John's* was the Revd. W.H. Hutton, the historian and biographer.

During Roland's sojourn as an undergraduate at Oxford he became deeply influenced by the Anglo-Catholic faculty at Pusey House, across the street from St. John's. Its Principal was

---

[12] Vol. 7 (October 1892).

[13] Coincidentally, his great-grandson (another Roland Allen) was to be the *last* Secretary of the Origen Society, which wound up nearly a century later.

Charles Gore, later Bishop of Oxford, and one of the founders of the so-called 'Liberal Catholic' tradition among High Anglicans; he edited the seminal collection of studies, *Lux Mundi* (1889). Father Philip Waggett, SSJE, an eminent sacramental theologian, was another inspiration for Roland; and he was particularly influenced by Pusey's librarian, the great liturgical scholar F. E. Brightman, whom he later referred to as his *dear Father in God*. One of Brightman's particular interests was the spirituality of the Eastern Churches, and it has been argued that this may account for Roland's own very Church-centred view of mission.[14]

It was under the influence of these Tractarian mentors, more than that of his devout mother at the other end of the Anglican spectrum, that Roland went after graduation to the High Anglican clergy training school in Leeds. Nevertheless, as Paton remarks, Roland's was always *the now old-fashioned Anglican Catholicism—sober, restrained, scholarly, immensely disciplined. There is no trace anywhere in him of the preoccupation with secondary matters of ceremony into which the high Tractarian position sometimes degenerated.*[15] Moreover, he was always to combine with his High Church emphasis on the Church and the Sacraments an Evangelical concern with a biblical foundation for any arguments and, above all, with the central importance of the Holy Spirit.

His motives when he went to clergy school were not complex: *When I was ordained, I was a child. My idea was to serve God in His Temple. Chiefly that, with a conviction that to be ignorant of God's Love revealed in Christ was to be in a most miserable state.* He impressed the Principal of the School as being *a refined intellectual man, small not vigorous, in no way burly or muscular . . . academic and fastidious rather . . . learning and civilization are more to him than to most men.*[16]

---

[14]See e.g. Talltorp, *op. cit.*, p. 11 and, above, footnote 3, p. viii.

[15]Paton, *Reform of the Ministry, op. cit.*, p. 24.

[16]Winfred Burrows (later Bishop of Chichester) in a letter to the Society for the Propagation of the Gospel in support of Roland's application in 1892.

In 1892 he was ordained deacon by Bishop Westcott of Durham; and a year later he became a priest. He served his curacy in the Durham diocese, in the parish of St. John the Evangelist, Darlington. But this was consciously no more than a prelude to service in the overseas mission field.

'In 1892 he was ordained Deacon.'
Roland Allen, c. 1892

CHAPTER II

First Years in China

**'they may be useful to the Church as Catechists,
or in some similar capacity'
Roland Allen with Clergy School pupils, Peking c. 1899**

When I was about four years old and heard that there were men who had never been told the Gospel, recounted Roland in his old age, he had cried out: *Then I shall go and tell them.*[1] At Oxford he had been actively considering missionary service and by now he was *simply thirsting to go.*

The Principal of his clergy school commented that *He is not the sort of man to impress settlers or savages by his physique*; and the

---

[1]This and the remark about his vocation in the last chapter may be found in Paton, *The Ministry of The Spirit, op. cit.,* p. 206.

Society for the Propagation of the Gospel (SPG) to which he first applied, turned him down on learning of his mysterious heart ailment. Undaunted by this rejection, in 1893 he applied to one of SPG's associated missions, the independent Church of England Mission to North China.[2] As in the parent body, the selectors for this mission expressed grave doubts. However, Roland managed successfully to argue that if he were going to die early he might just as well do so in the mission field: *If, as you say,* he challenged the examining doctor, *I have so bad a heart that I am likely to die soon, can you tell me why I should be likely to die sooner in China than in England?*

There seemed to be no answer to this; so he was accepted by the Mission the following year, although he did not leave for China until he had fully completed his curacy. In 1895, at the end of January, he set sail; and on March 22nd he arrived in Tientsin, whence Bishop Charles Perry Scott reported that:

> *We have been cheered since the ice broke up by the arrival first, of the Rev. Roland Allen and next, of Miss Wollaston and Nurse Sands, all of whom will, I expect, accompany us to Peking. Mr.Allen has been hard at work on the language for some five weeks.*[3]

In one of his very rare and economical autobiographical statements Roland relates that: *I went out to China in 1895, invited by Bishop Scott (of blessed memory) to open a clergy school for the diocese of North China . . . I spent 5 years learning the language and preparing some boys for work as catechists.*[4]

---

[2]The application and related papers are now deposited at Rhodes House. After Roland had been in China for 12 months, drawing no more than a stipend as acting chaplain to the British Legation, he was at last taken onto the payroll by SPG.

[3]*Quarterly Paper of the Mission of the Church of England in North China,* vol. III, pp. 17, 27, 48.

[4]Address to the Swanwick conference of the Church Missionary Society, printed in the *Church Missionary Review* (June 1927). *The North China Mission Quarterly* (October 1896) contains his 'First Impressions', pp. 53-56.

Figure 1.

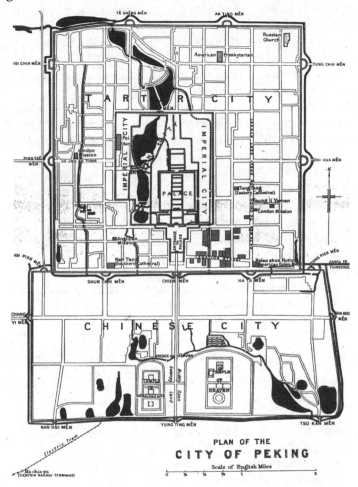

PLAN OF THE CITY OF PEKING [BEIJING] IN 1900.

(Reproduced from The Siege of the Peking Legations *by Roland Allen (Smith, Elder: 1901)*

The setting for those next five years of Roland's life is described vividly, but succinctly, and illustrated by a plan of the city (see Fig.1), in his account of *The Siege of the Peking Legations*. His evocative description of the approach to the city may be of particular interest to those who know modern Beijing:

> *The railway station,* Ma Chia Pu, *at which one arrives from Tientsin, is about one and a half miles outside the South Wall of the Chinese city. From that place an electric tram used to run to the central gate of the South Wall, the* Yung Ting Mên. *The contrast between the gaudy red and yellow car and the old grey wall before which it stops is most striking. It seems to illustrate the successful resistance of ancient obstruction . . .*

> *The wall of the Chinese city is not sufficiently great to be imposing, whilst it is sufficiently high to hide all view of the city inside from the newcomer. He is, therefore, often surprised when he has passed the little group of houses and shops which cling round the gate to find himself once more in open country, with the city, the real city, full in view, still about two miles away. The road from the* Yung Ting Mên *to the Tartar city runs straight as a pen, to use the Chinese expression, before him—a raised road, on either side of which is a broad expanse of muddy, swampy land, untilled and bare, over which wander a few thin sheep, plucking at the scanty tufts of rank grass. The soil is sprinkled with a white salt, which, in the hollows where water has been standing, forms little patches as though the place was cursed with the scab. On the right hand, at a little distance from the road-way, is the wall of a great enclosure, the compound within whose inmost heart lies the great Altar of Heaven, the centre of the Empire's worship, surrounded by many great shrines and temples, with gorgeous blue roofs, itself bare, roofed only by the blue sky . . . Opposite to it, on the left-hand side of the road, is another enclosure, smaller than the first, but yet of great extent, the Temple of Agriculture.*

24

After passing these two great temples the road rises over a bridge across a little stream feeding some great ponds in which goldfish, the toys and pets of the Chinese people, are cultivated. Or, if the season is dry, the road goes round the bridge and through the bed of the stream—for the Chinese carter prefers the soft earth to the steep stone incline of the bridge— and then plunges at once into the shops and busy life of the Chinese city. Yet, viewed from this point it seems rather as if the city was still before the traveller and that these busy quarters were only a suburb. This feeling is due to the dominating influence of the vast gate which lies right before him, the Ch'ien Mên, which towers up to heaven and seems to bar all advance rather than to invite approach. It is still nearly a mile distant, yet it proclaims in a voice of thunder that here is the city of the Ruler of the world; outside, small men may build their houses like swallows' nests round an old manorial tower, but within alone there is a city of princes.

Slowly the new-comer works his way down the great paved street choked with men and carts, hemmed in on either side with booths, by which the merchants, whose shops lie behind, seem to be struggling to press nearer and nearer to the centre of the tide, to thrust themselves upon the notice of the passer-by; then under a triumphal arch and over a great marble bridge which spans the moat, a bridge of three roads, down the centre one of which no carts or chairs pass except those of the Emperor. When he is not using it, it is occupied by a host of beggars and peddlers, whence it gets its popular name of 'The Beggars' Bridge'. Originally it was a splendid and interesting structure of solid white marble ornamented with dragons' heads and other carved work, but the dirt of ages has now sullied the purity of the marble and the neglect of ages has suffered the carving to fall into decay.

Immediately behind the bridge is the central gate; but that is closed. All ordinary traffic must make its way round

the great semicircle of the gate and enter either on the east or
west under smaller gate-towers and so into the enceinte, *to*
the huge tunnel which forms the entrance through the Tartar
wall itself. This tunnel and the gate-tower over it were once
among the chief glories of Peking. The massive building of
that solid unadorned archway, its deep gloomy shadows, the
huge red wooden pillars and the overhanging eaves of the
green-tiled roofs of the gate-tower above, formed a picture at
which the oldest resident in Peking was never tired of
gazing. The ceaseless traffic below, the undisturbed calm
above, impressed the mind with an almost painful sense of
the fluctuations of human life and the enduring influence of
the past. It was a sight not fully understood at first; the full
weight of its deep significance was only felt after many
visits. For my own part, the Ch'ien Mên *impressed me on*
the day that I left Peking more deeply than ever it had done
in the five years of my life in that city. That gate and the
Altar of Heaven seemed to me the most suggestive and awe-
inspiring that I had seen in the country.

Within the gate was an open square surrounded with a
stone railing, which I once heard irreverently compared to a
cattle-market. [This has nowadays become notorious as
'Tian-an-Men Square'.] *It was, like all things in China,*
neglected and desolate, its huge flag-stones interspersed with
weeds, its stone lions which crouch before the red gate
leading into the palace, and the gate itself, dirty and moss-
grown. Into this enclosure no-one was supposed to enter; but
on warm days it was dotted with beggars and idlers sprawl-
ing in the sun or loitering about . . .

From this enclosure east and west ran the Chiao Min
Hsiang, *or 'Street of Intercourse with the People', so named*
because here first the Chinese were allowed to reside within
the Tartar city. The east Chiao Min Hsiang *was later*
known to foreigners as the 'Legation Street', because here the
foreign Ministers all gathered . . .

Roland goes on to describe in some detail the topography of this Legation quarter, which was, of course, the setting for his account of the siege (see Fig.2). He then turns to the multiplicity of Christian missions:

> *The Roman Catholics had three large centres . . . the*
> Pei-T'ang, *or Northern Cathedral, inside the Imperial City*
> *to the north-west . . . the* Tung T'ang, *or East Cathedral, to*
> *the north of the Austrian Legation on the east side of the*
> *Imperial City . . . the* Nan T'ang, *or South Cathedral, just*
> *inside the southwest gate of the Tartar City . . .*
>
> *The American Presbyterians had a large compound in*
> *the north of the city; the London Mission had two com-*
> *pounds, one in the east, another in the west just inside the*
> P'ing Tsê Mên; *the American Board Mission was in the*
> *east; and in the south-east, close to the* Ha Ta Mên, *in the*
> Hsiao Shun Hu-tung, *was the large compound of the*
> *American Episcopal Methodists Mission . . .*
>
> *The Anglican Mission, of which I was in charge, was in*
> *the West City, a little to the north of the* Nan T'ang. *There*
> *were two compounds—one containing the church, bishop's*
> *house, deaconesses' house, and clergy house; the other*
> *containing the hospital and some houses inhabited by*
> *converts. Numerically it was a very small mission compared*
> *with most of the others in Peking.*[5]

Roland at once made friends with the Chinese, and *in spite of the great summer heat*, as the Bishop reports, he began to learn Mandarin quickly and well: in only a few years he was already distinguished as a '3,000-character man' and was preaching in Chinese. (This fluency was one reason that Bishop Scott was later to put forward his name for preferment as Bishop for the new see at Shantung.)

---

[5]*The Siege of the Peking Legations* (London: Smith Elder, 1901), pp. 28-41.

Roland also took over a day school for non-Christians in the neighbourhood, which had been started the previous year by the Revd. H.V. Norman. What is more, *no second priest could be spared to help Mr. Allen, on whose shoulders rested the Legation Chapel and the English congregation there, as well as the supervision of the printing press . . .*[6]

Besides all these tasks, he found time to write a few contributions for the Mission's quarterly journal, The Land of Sinim,[7] of which many are marked by the dry, sometimes acerbic, always self-deprecating humour, which in later years was often to puzzle and bewilder readers accustomed only to high seriousness, at least when matters of importance were under discussion. In an account of his *First Impressions of the Mission at Peking*, for example, he describes the small girls school and concludes drily that: *I should not like to see it inspected by one of Her Majesty's Inspectors of Schools*. In a description of the head printer's wedding, he ruefully records:

> *I had never used chopsticks, or eaten Chinese before, but I managed to get down enough to save my face, and to make myself feel rather sick . . . I left them to feed by themselves, and came away, nearly melted with the heat, and feeling very queer inside, and did no work for the rest of the day, for I thought a Chinese wedding a very tiring performance.*

These lighthearted commentaries, however, were almost all that Roland was prepared to write. *I suppose formally I ought to be sending you a report,* he remarks in a letter to Tucker, the SPG Mission Secretary, *but I have nothing to report.*

Although during the following summer Roland had a sharp attack of fever, and had to spend more than a month recuperat-

---

[6]Frank L. Norris, *China*, Mobray's series of *Handbooks of English*, no. 3.

[7]This was the title given, from the beginning of 1896, to the *Quarterly Papers of the Mission of the Church of England*, in connection with 'Bishop Scott's Special Fund' and the 'North China Diocesan Fund': the allusion is to the book of Isaiah 49:12 (A.V.)—'Sinim' was thought to be China. Citations in this Chapter are from that journal, unless otherwise indicated.

ing at St. Hilary's House of Rest in the Western Hills, his health in fact gave no serious cause for concern. And so, when the boys' school had been transferred to the care of Mr. Norman in Yung-Ch'ing, Roland was able to start on his principal task: in the Mission's annual report for 1897, we read that:

> *The opening of the college at Peking for the training of Chinese youths for the Native Ministry of the Church is the first subject of permanent interest. It is under the care of the Rev. Roland Allen, and it is earnestly hoped that his health may stand the strain of the work, and that good fruit may result from it.*[8]

In his Christmas letter the Bishop noted that: *Mr. Allen, I am very glad to record, opened his first Theological Class a month ago, and is hard at work, and greatly interested in the same.*

There were eight students in Roland's new class; the Bishop thought that *they may be useful to the Church as Catechists, or in some similar capacity, if not as ordained clergy.* Roland's own opinions were still very orthodox, and give no hint of the revolutionary ideas that he was later to express in *Missionary Methods* and other writings: *I do not think the Mission ought to be satisfied with less than a year's training in theology proper after the preparation before the student can be licensed as a catechist; and again another and longer period before the diaconate.*

Among other subjects, the clergy school programme included study of the first three centuries of Church history. *In this last they take a good deal of interest,* reported Roland, *especially in certain translations which I am making of portions of the Apostolic Fathers. My teacher who translates for me got quite excited over the letter of the Smyrnaeans concerning the death of Polycarp.*

Roland—*an able and devoted teacher* [9]—was from the first awake to new ideas and techniques. He procured a camera, and used the photographs in teaching, as well as to help the work of

---

[8] North China Mission, *Annual Report for 1897*, p. 3.

[9] Norris, *op.cit.*

the missionary society back home. In Peking he was obliged to develop and print his own work; and he even taught himself sufficient chemistry to be able to make unobtainable developing fluid. Tantalizingly, although many of his photographs of places and people still survive, none of them have any notes to indicate their subjects, apart from a few of those taken during and after the siege.

In her first impressions of the mission station, the future Deaconess Jessie Ransome recounts how: *Mr. Allen exhibited the magic lantern to the Chinese women and children, and afterwards it was shown in the preaching room . . . He is very anxious to get more sacred slides as he thinks they would be a most valuable means of teaching.*

He also demonstrated commitment to the principle of participatory teaching, by introducing debates on current affairs. To begin with *no speech, excluding the foreigners', exceeded two minutes, or about six sentences;* but by the end of the first year he could report that *They have notice now of a ten-minute limit. That is a wonderful change since this time last year, when the limit was ten words. But K'ang-Yu-Wei and the reformers, and the Empress and her crew have helped us wonderfully, and I have heard this term what I scarcely dared hope for a year ago, a real political debate. But I suppose we can scarcely expect a revolution every month, and it needs that to make them read the newspapers.*

Roland's young pupils made so much progress that he was able to observe, regarding their first examinations, that most of them *rather surprised me by their grasp of the situation and clear reproduction of the argument. My first question, 'Analyse from memory the first three chapters of the Epistle to The Ephesians', was really creditably done by two or three boys.*

A year later he and the Bishop decided to send out three of the trainees for practical work in the field as catechists; as the Bishop remarked in his quarterly letter to The Land of Sinim:

this will serve to prevent their becoming mere book-worms, give them some knowledge of men and things, and test their capacity both for evangelistic work and for bearing responsibility.

Regarding two of them Roland had doubts that they could ever progress beyond being catechists; and it was anticipated that one of these would not return to the clergy school. But the third boy, Wang Shu Ti'en (who had been appropriately christened 'Timothy'), was expected, if his practical experience went well, *to continue his studies here, in the hope that at the end of a second two years' course he may be ordained deacon.* This lad Roland was encouraging to work on a life of Saint Paul—the first such life, he believed, to be published in Chinese.

The first reports sent back by these students were encouraging, and so Roland could report: *I was glad to get such a bright account, because it is hard for young workers to be plunged at once into the depression of apparent failure, and any work which my boys try to do in Peking is of the most hopeless nature.*

All these tasks kept Roland himself almost continuously in the city of Peking, although early in 1898 he used the opportunity of the Chinese New Year vacation to visit the families of some of his pupils, who lived at Yung-Ch'ing, some 50 miles to the south; and later that year he spent a month in Chefoo, and was sent across to Wei-Hai-Wei by Bishop Scott to report on the potential for extending church work to that important naval base. Wei-Hai-Wei had just been leased by China to the British in return for their payment to the Japanese of an indemnity exacted by the latter after their victory over the Chinese in 1895. A condensed version of Roland's report appears in The Land of Sinim.

Early in the year 1900 he accompanied Bishop Scott to the annual Bishops' Conference in Tientsin; and he went on from there to observe the work of Ningpo Clergy College under Bishop Moule. Just before Lent he also made a rail journey round the Gulf of Pechili to Niu-Chang (where he had the misfortune to fall and break his collar-bone, while crossing a river at night).

Notwithstanding all these activities, and his heavy load of responsibilities in Peking, Roland was already beginning to think deeply about fundamental questions relating to the propagation of the Church. When first he took up his post at the clergy school, *I was quite innocent: I did not question the propriety of such a course for a moment. . . During those five years I became more and more uneasy in my mind.*[10]

The sort of thing that worried him was to hear such a remark as that made by another Christian worker in China, that the missionary as an evangelist was usually a failure, and so should concentrate on straightforward school teaching: *the foreign missionary must seek a field of employment, a branch of work which is more adapted to him, which he can do better than any native.*[11]

However, for the time being Roland kept most such doubts to himself. His name was even put forward for consecration as Bishop for the proposed new diocese of Shantung, although he was still at the time less than the requisite thirty years old. But the authorities decided—no doubt providentially—not to act on this recommendation; and meanwhile Roland continued his teaching and other work in the Chinese capital.

---

[10]*Church Missionary Review, op.cit.*
[11]The Rev. James Jackson in *The Chinese Recorder,* January 1893, pp. 7-8.

CHAPTER III

The Gathering Storm

'his vantage point in the Anglican Mission'

From his vantage point in the Anglican Mission, as well as during his daily visits to the British Legation, Roland was well placed to observe the rising tide of resentment against all foreign intrusion that was beginning to sweep through China, where he noted *a deep-rooted conviction that the European intruders are men possessed of might, but destitute of any true sense of right, that their objects are not honest, nor their means praiseworthy.*[1]

Although Western commercial and territorial greed were seen as the primary reasons for this Chinese xenophobia, an element of it was also a growing mistrust for Western missionary activities: *It was not that they hated the Christian religion* qua *religion; they hated it* qua *foreign.* What is more, they felt it to be an upstart newcomer; as Roland was later to remark:

> *The Chinese are apt to compare the antiquity of their religion with the modern character of ours . . . If Christianity is to be presented acceptably to the Chinese, surely it ought to be through Chinese teachers who have remained Chinese in thought and education, but whose Chinese thought is permeated with Christian doctrine and belief. So one might find an Apostle.*[2]

Another blemish in some of the missions in Chinese eyes — notoriously the French and German Roman Catholics whose *bishops and priests began to assume the style of great mandarins*— was that they were ready to intervene on behalf of their converts, even if these were law-breakers. Criminals, it was alleged, *often joined the Christian Church solely in order to escape the arm of the law by sheltering themselves under the* aegis *of a powerful guild which the local officials dared not offend . . . No matter whether he did good or evil, he ceased to be subject to the law and authority of the national Goverment.*

The Anglican bishops were worried by this state of affairs. At their conference in Shanghai in September 1899 they tried to dissociate themselves from such presumptive and provocative behaviour:

---

[1]These and other extracts in this and the following chapter, unless otherwise indicated, come from three sources: Roland's three articles in *The Cornhill Magazine* of November and December 1900, and February 1901; his book on *The Siege of the Peking Legations;* and Jessie Ransome's diary *The Siege Hospital in Peking.*

[2]Article on 'The Chinese Character and Missionary Methods' in *The East & the West* (July 1903), pp. 317-329.

We have no wish to complicate our spiritual responsibilities by the assumption of political rights and duties such as have been conceded to the Roman Catholic hierarchy. But we cannot view without alarm, both on behalf of our own flock and the Chinese population generally, the rapidly growing interference of French and other Roman Catholic priests with the provincial and local government of China.

But to the vast majority of Chinese *all foreigners were Christians, and all Christians were to be judged by the actions of those whom they happened to meet.* You may add to these, if you will, the conduct of foreign merchants and engineers travelling in the interior, which was not always an excellent example of the practice of Christianity.

We may note in passing that Roland, even so early as this, was beginning to feel concern about the potential impact of 'non-professional missionaries'—of lay persons such as Western merchants and engineers—all of whom were assumed by their host countries' populations to be Christians, simply because they were the fellow-nationals of 'professional' missionaries. It seems reasonable to speculate that it was Roland's anxieties that gave rise to an editorial in the July 1900 number of The Land of Sinim, in which it is noted that:

[Europeans] may be Jews or avowed Atheists; many of them may never mention the name of their God except in profanity and blasphemy; perhaps some may be leading a life far more degraded than that of the lowest amongst the Chinese: but, for all that, in the eyes of the Chinese they are Christian, and, for good or evil, another God, another Creed, another philosophy, another ideal, is aggressively forced upon the Chinese mind.

Droughts and floods at this time helped to consolidate popular belief among the Chinese that Heaven was angered by *the presence of foreigners and the evil influence of the foreign doctrine.* The Empress Dowager and most of her ministers were happy to lend support to this view, for fear that otherwise some demagogues might well encourage the people to challenge her own high-handed behaviour. Moreover, international events were at that time showing that after all these Europeans were not omnipotent: *We sorely need one or two great victories in the Transvaal to restore our good name out here,* wrote Roland; *At present the Chinese are fond of comparing England to China, the Transvaal to Japan, and fancy that we shall go to pieces as they did . . .*

In March 1900 threatening placards began to appear on the streets of several big cities in China. A literal translation of one of these demonstrates why missionaries like Roland, isolated from the foreign legations at his clergy school in the Anglican mission compound in the southwest of Peking's Inner (or Tartar) City, had reason to feel worried:

> *All the Christian Churches notice. We set one week's time.*
> *All the Churches must be converted into Immortal Halls, or*
> *the members must leave them. If you disobey, we will pull*
> *down the buildings with our magic arts or burn them down*
> *with fire. Then repentance will be beyond your reach.*
>
> *(Signed:)*
>
> *The Righteous Harmony*
> *Fist Society of the Empire.*[3]

In this signature appears translated the name of a semi-religious society, for which the European nickname was 'the Boxers'. This had originally been established nearly a century earlier, in the reign of the Emperor Chia Ch'ing, to rally people for mutual defence—*to support the cause of peace and righteousness, if necessary by force.* In the face of the new alien aggression, its members now *proclaimed themselves the Heaven-designated deliverers of their country from the foreign yoke.*

We are concerned here only with the figure of Roland Allen, so no attempt will be made to discuss and analyse in any detail *those incidents which have never been surpassed in modern days,*

---

[3]*Peking & Tientsin Times*, March 31, 1900.

certainly since the horrors of the Indian Mutiny.[4] The first atrocity
wrought by the Boxer movement which called itself to attention
outside China was when one of Roland's fellow Anglican priests,
the Revd. Sidney Brooks, was murdered on the last day of 1899.
Even after this event, most diplomats were still wont to dismiss
the potential threat to the foreign community as negligible.
Roland, however, remarked that *men more closely in touch with the
Chinese people could not fail to observe that there was a change in the
moral atmosphere, such as they had never felt before.* The indigenous
Chinese Christians gave warning to missionaries of all denominations that *This danger will not blow over.* So the missionaries as
well as their converts began to take precautions accordingly.

Roland urged the elderly Confucian who was teaching him
the classics to stop running the risk of coming daily to teach him:

> *You are not a convert; you are not a Christian;* he pointed
> out: *If a disturbance breaks out . . . you will be liable to
> persecution or perhaps to death, and not only yourself but
> your whole family will be in considerable danger.*

> *We have always been very good friends,* replied the old
> man: *I find nothing in my conscience or in my religious
> books to tell me I have been doing anything wrong in coming
> here to teach you . . . I shall continue to come to your house
> until you tell me you will not have me . . . If I am punished
> for it, that has nothing whatever to do with me, because I am
> doing what is right.*

> *He is a better man than I am,* noted Roland, recounting
> this story, *but I have something to tell him he does not
> know! . . .'You know nothing about sin, or your relationship
> to God'.*[5]

Outside Peking things were going from bad to worse. A
young American Presbyterian missionary, the Revd. W.B. Stelle,

---

[4] Editorial in *The Land of Sinim*, No.VIII/4 (October 1900), p. 5.

[5] S.P.G. (Society for the Propatgation of the Gospel), *Report of the Bicentenary*,
p. 139.

recounted to Roland a thrilling venture by himself and one Dr. Anent of the American Board Mission *alone, armed with revolvers, into the heart of a district seething with Boxer agitation, in order to encourage their converts . . . They heard of places all round them being pillaged, and their fellow-Christians ruined, maltreated, mutilated, murdered . . . It was no wonder* mused Roland, already beginning to foreshadow some of the ecumenical ideas that he would develop later, *that missionaries like these, ready to lay down their lives for their people, exercised a great influence and won converts to the fold . . . It made me feel doubly sad at the divisions of Christendom which separate from communion men who so jeopardize their lives for the name of the Lord Jesus.*

In Peking itself, nothing appeared to come of the Boxers' threats, so the diplomatic corps continued to make light of them, and to rely on assurances of friendship from the Imperial Court. On 19th May the Catholic Bishop and Vicar Apostolic in Peking addressed to the French Ambassador a long and anxious letter, detailing numerous atrocities and threats in other parts of China: *De jour en jour la situation devient plus grave et plus menaçante . . .*, he warned: *La persecution religieuse n'est qu'un rideau; le but principal est l'extermination des Européens* [6]. . . But even this authoritative plea failed to stir the foreign diplomats to any decisive action.

It was only the burning of Fêngt'ai railway station, and the destruction of the bridge at Lu Kou Ch'iao on May 28, 1900, in Roland's view, that *as I believe, preserved us all from having our throats cut*—because these acts at last persuaded the foreign ambassadors to bring in their own guards. That same evening a messenger came over to the Anglican Mission from the British Legation (the Embassy compound), located about two miles away in the southeast part of the Tartar city, *to say that in view of the gravity of the situation they would receive any British subjects who wished to take refuge.*

---

[6] 'Day by day the situation is growing more serious and more threatening . . . The religious persecution is no more than a veil: the principal objective is the extermination of the Europeans.'

Roland had been left in charge at Peking when Bishop Scott departed in mid-April on a visitation to mission stations in South Chihli and Shantung. By this time they had several British companions at the Mission. Besides the Bishop and his wife, there were Jessie Ransome, who had been recruited a year after Roland, and had been running St. Faith's Home for women in the same compound as the clergy school; Jessie's sister, Edith;[7] and a hospital nurse, Miss Lambert. The Ransome sisters had both been 'solemnly set apart' as Deaconesses by Bishop Scott.

So when the message came from the British Legation, *I at once decided to accept the offer*, wrote Roland:

> *There were with me in the compound the Bishop's wife Mrs.*
> *Scott, two deaconesses and a nurse. I kept one deaconess,*
> *who indeed would have refused to go, to look after the*
> *Chinese women and children who yet remained under our*
> *care . . . and sent them all off in carts that night. Deaconess*
> *Jessie Ransome and myself were left alone in charge of the*
> *mission.*

Anxious about having many helpless women and girls on their hands (for the Boxer movement had become notorious for kidnapping marriageable girls), Roland and Jessie arranged to send them all away from Peking *by twos and threes, going different ways so as not to attract attention.* Mercifully the railway line to Tientsin was still open, because the Boxers, having killed the man in the ticket office and burned all his tickets, characteristically supposed that these actions would prevent any possible escape by train!

Roland was in a quandary, for—although he continued to assure his Chinese pupils and the mission servants that *I shall stay so long as I can be of any use*—he knew very well that staying in the event of any real trouble would not only be of no use, but might well provoke the Boxers to attack: *That sort of thing gave*

---

[7]The deaconesses' elder brother was a Professor in Leeds; and their younger one, Arthur, later became a well-known author, especially of children's books (notably the *Swallows and Amazons* series).

one a pain in the pit of the stomach and another in the top of the head . . .

Anyway, he and Deaconess Jessie both prepared for the worst. Indeed, they found such preparations to be the best tonic: *The moment that any real action was to be taken, any work to be done, any scheme however risky to be executed, or even only planned, that feeling disappeared.*[8]

Helped and advised by Dr. Gilbert Reid, an experienced American neighbour, who had been a Presbyterian missionary, the two Anglicans prepared to disguise themselves in Manchu clothes, and to take with them in two carts the two old women and two children who were their only companions now left in the clergy school. *The plan was to drive about the streets all night with the curtains down, and at daybreak to attempt to pass out of one of the east gates, and so to Tientsin either by road or river . . .* It will be seen from the plan of the city (Fig.1) that the direct route to join their British companions in the Legation would have led them through the dense crowds and past the hostile guards at the Ch'ien Mên gate; and that the only alternative was to travel along quieter roads north, east and south all the way round the Imperial City, a journey of several hours. Moreover, *To get carters willing to run the risk of transporting foreigners might not be easy; to make sure that they would fulfil their contract rather than secure their own lives by betraying us, was still less easy.*

The safe arrival of a company of nearly four hundred foreign troops temporarily calmed everyone's fears. However, in the mission compounds, *The Chinese thought otherwise, and continued their packing.* The deaconess noted that they *pawned all their best clothes and anything they set value on, so that the greater part of their property has been converted into pawn tickets, which are easily portable property!* Meanwhile Roland and his companions, fearful not so much of a general rising as of *an incursion of thieves and vagabonds* during the general unrest in the city, every night

---

[8]Preface to *Educational Principles & Missionary Methods, op. cit.*, p. ix. We may note in passing how reminiscent this is of Roland's father's subject of study—St. John Chrysostom: *Preaching makes me well; as soon as I open my mouth to speak my weariness is all forgotten.*

kept watches in regular order armed with our one pistol.

On June 2nd a burned and blistered Chinese Anglican came running wearily into the mission compound to say he had escaped the previous day from a Boxer attack in Yung-Ch'ing, a town about 50 miles to the south. Very soon more refugees arrived, with news that one of the two Anglican missionaries there had been killed, and the other captured; and only a day or two later it was confirmed that he, too, had been killed, along with at least eighteen Chinese converts. The Boxers used the baptismal register to track them down.

When to all this was added news that the mission doctor had died at sea of *a kind of apoplectic seizure*, we can feel sympathy for the anxiety in Jessie Ransome's diary; in a single year, she noted:

> *Six members of the Mission have gone from earth to Paradise . . . and three by violent deaths. Who will be next?*
> However, when *Our cook, a heathen, told me solemnly this morning that he thought we had much better go to Japan for awhile . . . I told him I had no intention of moving at present.*

Roland was beginning to feel rather overwhelmed. So when he learned that Bishop Scott and his companion, Mr. Norris,[9] had got back safely to Tientsin after their travels, he arranged for Mrs. Scott to take the train and join her husband; and he sent a telegram to ask that Mr. Norris should come to Peking without delay. Norris duly arrived on Whit Sunday, June 3rd, on the last train to get through to Peking, and *was thus shut in the city in time to be of inestimable value during the siege as a leader of barricade-builders . . . The Marines said of him that he was a man who feared neither bullets, devils, nor stinks; others noticed that his barricades were straight, upright, and strong . . .*

All this time, reports Roland, *I had been endeavouring to preserve the ordinary routine of school work.* The three young men still remaining were a Shantung boy called Shih Hung Chang;

---

[9]The Rev'd. Frank L. Norris, later himself to become the Bishop in North China.

Lei Yü Ch'ün, from Tai Wang Chuang; and Wang Shu T'ien, who came from Yung-Ch'ing itself, where his father and mother were known as good Christians. All three were horrified when Roland told them of the deaths of his fellow missionaries:

> *They loved Mr. Norman as a father. 'We must have our revenge,' I said 'and it is you who have to take it. There is only one revenge a Christian man knows, and that is to preach the Gospel to those who have wronged him. It is your business, not mine. Open your books. . .' They opened their books, took notes, wrote me essays as if there was nothing wrong in the world at all . . .*[10]

At Evensong, Jessie recalled, they sang *'For all the Saints'* and *Mr. Allen preached to us about the present danger and how we ought to meet it; beautiful, helpful words about the hope that is set before us, to which a violent death may be but a shorter road.*

However, when news came through that members of their own families were being forced to burn incense to idols, all the three students asked to be allowed to go and join them in their hour of need. Reluctantly, Roland and Norris helped them to devise as safe a plan as possible for their escape from Peking, although:

> *Chinese say that a Christian has a Christian smell, and that a Christian can be marked at sight by his countenance.*
> *It was quite open to question whether they would ever reach home or if they did whether anything but martyrdom awaited them . . . In the face of what I considered was certain death, he* [Wang Shu T'ien, the Yung-Ch'ing boy] *went, in order to tell those people that they must die rather than deny Jesus Christ! Whilst the Church has amongst her members such Christians as these,* exulted Roland, *she cannot fail to make progress—she must win the world.*
>
> *Thus my school was broken up,* he concluded, *and I felt that my work was done.*

---

[10]S.P.G., *op, cit.,* p. 140.

CHAPTER IV

The Siege of the Peking Legations[1]

'the chaplain's pastoral duties'

On June 7th 1900 the Anglican mission received messages from the British Legation with instructions that all British *women* should now go and stay there, and that the Mission compound should be handed over to the local police, whilst preparations were made for a siege that might last as long as a fortnight.

---

[1]This is the title of the book about the Siege that was subsequently written by Roland to raise money for the Mission. As noted earlier, most of the citations in this and the preceding chapter are taken either from that book or from Jessie Ransome's siege diary.

Roland and Frank Norris duly complied: *About 9.30 p.m. the officials, three or four stupid and sluggish mandarins, arrived, and Mr. Norris solemnly handed over the compound to their charge, and we came away.* The deaconesses were allowed to bring with them their remaining charges, a Manchu convert named Miss Hung, and two little orphans from Chefoo.

At the Legation, of course, Roland already had the status of Chaplain to the British diplomatic mission. On Trinity Sunday, June 10th, a great parade service was held in the *T'ing-'rh* (pavilion) in front of the Minister's house, because the chapel was too small to hold the unwonted crowd. *A temporary altar was placed at one end, and covered with the Union Jack, and the cross and vases placed upon it, so as to make a little bit of a church-like effect,* recounts Deaconess Jessie; but *there was no need for any outward accessories to increase the solemnity and earnestness of our prayers and intercessions, not only for ourselves, but for 'all in anxiety at home'.*

Notwithstanding the recent deaths by violence of three of their fellow clergy, Roland and his colleague continued to go to visit the Mission every day, until the eve of the Boxer attack. Roland did concede that:

> *the incongruity of the situation reduced me to a state of helpless admiration. Here were we, walking unarmed through crowds of Chinese, who made way for us, as usual, without the slightest sign of hostility.*

Figure 2.

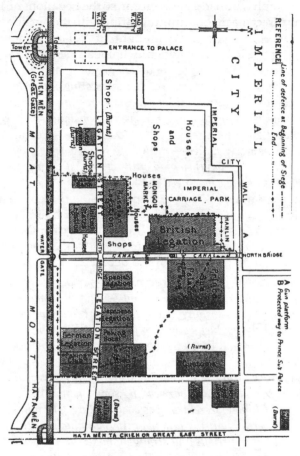

**PLANS OF THE LEGATION QUARTER,
AND OF THE BRITISH LEGATION
PEKING [BEIJING] 1900**

(Reproduced from The Siege of the Peking Legations *by Roland Allen (Smith, Elder: 1901)*

However, things were becoming more and more ominous. The telegraph wire had now been cut, so the Legations no longer had any direct means of communicating with the outside world. Not everyone would have thought of Roland's method of alleviating tension, but it evidently helped to soothe Deaconess Jessie's nerves: *Mr. Allen began to-day to give us a series of lectures on the Minor Prophets, which are most interesting and delightful . . .* Her sister, too, commented on *a most interesting one on Amos . . . with a wonderful application to present circumstances.*[2]

Roland gave lectures to the soldiers, too—presumably on rather less esoteric topics—and Jessie reports that they *are very much interested . . . [and] so glad of the chance of coming to church, that one feels the time here need not be wasted.*

At last, on June 20th, the Imperial Government issued an ultimatum, giving an impossible twenty-four hours for all the foreign embassies to evacuate Peking. It was clear that the real siege of the Legations was about to begin. Roland describes the frenzied final preparations for the defence:

It was a wonderful sight; everyone was slaving away with all his might. Mr. Dering, the Second Secretary, as master of the stables, was dashing about in his shirt, with his head tied up in a handkerchief, collecting fodder. M. Chamot, the hotel-keeper, and Fargo Squiers, the son of the American Secretary, who seemed to think the whole affair was a huge joke, drove furiously to and fro, bringing in stores of all kinds. Mr. Norris was barricading somewhere; Mr. Ker, the Second Chinese Secretary, was coal-hauling. The military people were organising and planning. Gradually little mountains of various and strangely mixed goods were collected in different parts of the Legation . . . Boxes, bundles, packing cases, were scattered everywhere in heaps. The place resembled nothing so much as the deck of an ocean liner just going out of dock . . .

Foreigners of every kind poured in from the outlying

---

[2]*The Land of Sinim*, Vol.VIII/4 (October 1900), p. 43.

missions and other parts of the city. *But time ran on apace: four o'clock, the hour at which the event was to declare itself, was close at hand . . . A small group of men gathered on the lawn, watch in hand, to await the expected moment. It reminded one of the Eights at Oxford. Five minutes more, three minutes more, two minutes more, and then firing was heard on the east . . . Serjeant Murphy rushed up and saluted.* 'Firing has begun, sir,' he said. *The real siege had begun.*

I shall not here attempt to re-tell the whole story of the grim events between that moment and the arrival of the relief column on August 14th; nor even to refer to all the many incidents that are brought to life most vividly in Granfer's and the Deaconess Jessie's published diaries. The siege itself has, after all, been exhaustively described in numerous historical studies.

In summary, Roland's part in the siege was principally to carry out the chaplain's pastoral duties, leading services as regularly as possible, and of course caring for the sick and the dying, and conducting funeral services. As well as these, his 'professional' duties, he worked—like every other able-bodied person—on helping to build and to shore up barricades; and he took his turn as one of the night-watchmen. Moreover, with his fluency in Chinese, he could be of service to the military: *I was sent with Captain Wray and a small guard to inquire into the meaning of a light which was burning at the sluice-gate under the Tartar wall,* he recounts early in the siege, before the Imperial troops had joined the Boxer assault; *That turned out to be the lantern of a Chinese guard set to prevent anyone coming into the Legation quarter by that way. The soldiers of the guard were perfectly friendly.* Miss Lambert had proved to be the only fully qualified and certificated nurse among the staff of the foreign legations: so when the siege began she was put in charge of their temporary hospital as Matron. Until Roland himself became seriously ill for three weeks with tonsilitis, he served as one of Miss Lambert's assistants in the hospital, which was housed in what were usually the Chancery offices of the Legation.

Roland's work in the hospital helped to bring home to him with renewed force the difficulties of intercultural

47

understanding. One such episode recounted by him about a Japanese soldier was also recorded by Deaconess Jessie:

One man—Kuchiki by name—was brought in during the early days of the siege with his knee absolutely smashed to pieces by a shell. It suppurated badly and was most painful . . . His bed was near a window; and one day, as he found the sun too hot on his head, and saw no one at hand to help him, he managed to shuffle himself completely round, with his feet where his head had been. Our chaplain, the Rev. R. Allen, who used to be constantly at the hospital, happened to go into the ward and inquired who had moved him. To his astonishment Kuchiki replied that he had moved himself, whereupon Mr. Allen gave him some pretty straightforward remonstrances on the danger of playing such tricks with a leg like his, and left the ward. Poor Kuchiki's English was not quite equal to the occasion. He saw that he had done something which did not meet with the approval of Mr. Allen, to whom he was devoted, and was determined to make matters all right again . . . and when, about ten minutes later, Mr. Allen again looked in, he found Kuchiki again lying with his head in the blazing sun, and a smile of conscious virtue on his face.

During the early phase of the siege, before the assassination of the German Ambassador, Baron von Ketteler, Roland and his companions maintained a truly remarkable *sang froid* in their pursuit of as normal a life as possible; one afternoon, for instance, after the burning of the great gate of the Tartar city:

I took one of the deaconesses and Miss Lambert for a walk upon the wall to see the ravages of the great fire. We went right up to the Ch'ien Mên without arms of any sort . . . to poke about amidst the ruins for tiles as mementoes of that great sight . . .

The besieged community found other pastimes, too. Roland records how much they appreciated the books belonging to their host, the First Secretary—Mr. Cockburn: *The library was not large, but it was extraordinarily catholic, ranging from law to the art of war, from the classics to yellow-backs. Every class of literature was represented—theology,* biography, *history,* belles-lettres, *science, art, novels, French and English. Every taste could find something to amuse and edify.*

The American missionaries *used to enliven the evenings by singing hymns and songs outside the chapel door. It was curious and entertaining to sit out in the dim twilight and listen to the strains of 'Hail, Columbia,' and 'Marching through Georgia,' or 'De Ringtailed Coon,' or 'Nearer, my God, to Thee,' to an accompaniment of rifle shots.*

Roland's affection for the Chinese, moreover, was undiminished: he used to chat to the Boxers over the ramparts during intervals between their assaults, and noted with pleasure how, after a day of fighting, the city watchman would still go his customary rounds, beating his rattle as usual:

> *To meet them on a dark night reminds one irresistibly of Dogberry and his friends, a lot of old ruffians clad in any sort of rough and grimy costume, shambling along with a lantern and a rattle, looking far more likely to discourage honest men than to terrify thieves . . . But the clang of their rattle, when once familiar, is a cheerful and homely sound . . . it spoke of a day which was gone, of quiet ordinary peace for civil men.*

Roland used to converse with the scholarly Mr. T'ang, the Legation's Head Writer, and these discussions *reopened in my mind the impossibility of the foreigner ever being in real sympathy with a people like the Chinese . . . I felt doubly disgusted when I heard people talk of the Boxers and the Chinese in one sweeping denunciation as devils and monsters of iniquity. They seemed to me to have done nothing morally worse than the French did at the Revolution, nothing morally worse than we ourselves did when we burnt witches alive; yet no-one would feel justified in condemning the whole French race as a race of devils or the whole English race as a race of monsters because in their ignorance they thought such iniquities to be just and lawful . . . Yet at that time if a man ventured to suggest such a thought there were people in the Legation who would refuse to speak to him.*

In his diary of the siege Roland never fails to spotlight the contribution of his Chinese companions. At one stage, for example, some trees were giving cover to enemy snipers. Consequently when Roland, who was looked upon as their pastor by the German Lutherans, went to accompany a funeral party to their Legation, *we had orders to cross the South Bridge at the double, for there was as yet no barricade to protect the road.*

To deal with this problem a Chinese catechist from the Methodist Mission *went out alone and hewed down these small trees in splendid style . . . He refused to allow a foreigner to go with him, saying:* 'They will shoot at you when they see you are a foreigner; they will not pay so much attention to me'. *Between his blows he interjected little prayers,* 'Christ, give me strength,' 'Lord, help me,' *and smote the tree with great effect . . . A day or two later I missed that man and heard with sorrow that he had been shot . . . I regret exceedingly that I neglected to record his name.*

Like all people under siege, Roland's dominant concerns, he later remarked, were with domestic preoccupations: the quantity and quality of the diminishing food supplies; and the difficulty of getting enough sleep, not least because of a plague of mosquitoes and flies. He shared the general admiration for the ingenuities of the French Legation's chef, who proved himself capable of working culinary miracles with ponies, mules, dogs, and even rats: *there was only one creature that he never succeeded in making palatable,* Granfer told me, *and that was cat.*

Patients in the hospital did remarkably well, according to Deaconess Jessie:

. . . there were wonderful blancmanges, fritters, pancakes, rice puddings—all made without eggs or milk, and yet, strange to say, quite palatable

. . . Sometimes, too, a little 'game' would be provided for some special invalid, in the shape of a magpie or a few sparrows . . .

Again, Roland pays tribute to his Chinese companions. After one major assault and fire, the staff returned to the ruined

50

kitchen, and served up meals as if nothing had happened. The cooking-stove was still there; what did it matter whether there were doors or windows?

After nights on watch, followed by days of incessant labour, Roland on one occasion became so tired that he fell asleep on a table on the verandah, and did not awaken, even when his comrades mounted a Nordenfelt machine gun on the other end of the table and fired over him! Deaconess Jessie's diary vividly describes the surrounding scene:

A horse was killed just in front of the verandah, and pieces of shells came into two of the wards. We could hardly hear ourselves speak, and the noise somehow seems to get onto my brain, so that even when it has ceased I still fancy I hear it. It is curious how used we get to going about with bullets whizzing about our heads; but I confess I do not like bomb-shells, there is something so 'skeary' about them, and the noise and flash are so bewildering.

In the First Secretary's house also, where Roland and his fellow Anglicans were living, life could be alarming: *Several bullets had found their way in: one had pierced a hat hanging on a peg a foot or two above one of the missionaries' beds, and some of the people were feeling nervous.*

The family still treasures a little brass tray that Roland was carrying around the hospital one day. Part of the rim is missing: it was knocked off by one of those *bullets whizzing about*, which otherwise would have penetrated his chest, if not his heart.

At times the weather was at least as ferocious as the enemy attack, as Roland vividly portrays:

I kept watch that night in the stable yard, huddled in a blanket under the projecting eaves of the stables . . . the rain pouring down in torrents, the night dark as pitch. Flashes of lightning of splendid brilliancy from time to time lit up the yard as if it were broad daylight, and kept one straining one's eyes into the darkness waiting for the next moment of glory, when the effort to take in every point in the picture in

*the twinkling of an eye was almost painful in its inten-
sity . . . In the intervals between the peals of thunder, bullets
sped over my head with every variety of song. I amused
myself with counting these, and trying to fix to each its
proper name: a fierce swish, a long sighing hiss, a terrible
ping; some made no noise at all until a crack and a splintered
tile or falling twigs showed where they struck.*

Yet in spite of all this Roland still had an eye for drama and
beauty amid tragedy. The fire at the great Ch'ien Mên gate was —

*one of the finest sights which man can conceive . . . when
once the fire had got firm hold within, the outside brickwork
acted like a funnel and the flames poured out at the top,
roaring, leaping, exulting like living things; whilst through
the windows and doors one could see a mass of bright red
flame glowing and thundering within. It was a sight to
remember and to dream of in night watches—a Buddhist hell
taken out of picture books and translated into reality.*[3]

As a scholar, Roland was truly appalled when the whole of
the beautiful Hanlin compound was utterly destroyed and its
unique library completely lost. *As usual throughout the siege,* he
remarks ruefully, *the people who had had least experience of China
judged best . . . The Hanlin was not to them a sacred place . . . The
experienced men trusted that the Chinese would respect their own
traditions. The inexperienced looked upon them as a barbarian, the
experienced as a civilised people. At this time the people acted as
barbarians and set fire to the place. It was a monstrous deed . . . At such
a moment no-one had leisure to look carefully over the vast stores of
books, to select, arrange, transport. Only a few fragments were
collected and gathered into a place of security.*

---

[3]Coincidentally, Roland's great-granddaughter, another Priscilla Allen,
was studying in Peking when the square beside this gate once again found its
modernized name notorious: Priscilla's task at that time was to convey to the
students occupying the Tian-an-Men Square details of the B.B.C.'s hourly news
bulletins.

Notwithstanding this vandalism, Roland's aesthetic senses were not dulled:

> *When I went up there in the evening, the fire was still burning, making a vast red glare against the deep blue of the Chinese evening sky; and one great tree . . . stripped of all foliage, stretched out its bare arms to heaven, burning with no flame but with a hollow translucent glow as if it had been cut out of a living ruby.*

On August 13th *the attack became exceedingly furious . . . About 9 p.m. there was a general call to arms, the bell rang furiously; every man not on duty rushed to the Bell Tower, and was given his post. Every weapon in the Legation was handed out. Even Mr. Norris and myself, who had never been armed before, were provided with revolvers . . . Then I sat out on the verandah of the house with the deaconesses, who could not sleep because of the deafening noise of the rifles and guns.*

But by dawn next morning this last effort of the enemy had clearly failed. Roland worked hard in the hospital until about 2 o'clock in the afternoon:

> *I had just gone to lie down for a short rest after the somewhat scanty sleep of the last night, when suddenly I heard cheering in the compound, and, rushing out, I saw Sikhs coming onto the lawn . . . Jessie was there too: Soon the whole compound was alive with picturesque Indian troops, Sikhs, Punjaub Infantry, Pathans, Cuttacks, and magnificent looking Bengal lancers; such a treat to see a real horse again.*

At home in England the anxious Secretary at the Mission's headquarters was delighted to receive this brief telegram from Bishop Scott: 'chefoo, 12.15 p.m. peking all five well, inform society, bishop' [4]

The allied troops, under Britain's General Gaselee, had at last reached Peking, and had lifted the siege. *That night the American missionaries ended their concert with the Doxology, and we all joined in.*

---

[4]*The Land of Sinim*, Vol.VIII/4 (October 1900), p. 77.

53

CHAPTER V

Furlough; and Engagement

'It was a howling wilderness'
The Anglican Mission in Peking, August 1900

Elsewhere in China well over 30,000 Christians had perished, including 135 missionaries of various denominations, together with over 50 of their children. During the Siege itself, 90 had been killed and over 130 wounded.[1] Yet Roland and his mission companions had all survived. *Some say we had extraordinary luck,* he remarks pensively, *But they are not the wise.*

As soon as possible after the relief, Roland and Frank Norris hurried over to visit their old mission compound:

We found a heap of ruins. The wall was broken down and the

---

[1]W.R. Williams, *Ohio Friends in the Land of Sinim* (Mount Gilead, Ohio: 1925), chapter VI—'China in Crisis'.

whole place levelled with the ground. It was a heap of broken bricks, in which it was difficult even to trace the ground plan of the houses . . . Nothing remained standing save parts of the walls of the clergy school and of the girls' school. Not a tree, not a stick, not a shrub survived. It was a howling wilderness . . . We went into the great pawnshop, in which all our Christians had deposited their treasures for safe keeping; it was deserted, looted, empty, and bare . . .

Sergeant Herring, the longest serving member of the British Legation staff, went to visit the foreign cemetery, west of the city, and returned with the news that the wall had been destroyed, the trees cut down, the tombstones broken, the graves rifled, the place utterly laid waste: *I can tell the graves, sir; I can't recognise men's bones,* said he to Roland.

As a matter of principle, SPG (the Society for the Propagation of the Gospel, parent society of the North China Mission) *decided neither to claim nor to accept any compensation from the China Government for damage to buildings or loss of life.*[2] So funds for reconstruction had to be sought in other ways. Most of the citations in the previous chapters are taken from Deaconess Jessie Ransome's *Story of the Siege Hospital in Peking; and from The Siege of the Peking Legations,* as Roland's own vivid book describing the episode is entitled.[3] By April 1901 both books were being sold by the North China Mission Association to raise money to make good the destruction caused not only by the Boxer rising, but also by its ruthless international suppression.

A less melancholy way for the missionaries to pass their time, whilst plans were being made for their journey home, was afforded by the opportunity to be amongst the first Europeans ever to penetrate the Forbidden City and to walk in the temple enclosures. Roland was especially impressed by the great circular altar of the Temple of Heaven, in its beautiful solitary simplicity:

---

[2]*Land of Sinim,* Vol. IX/3 (July 1901), p. 13.
[3]See favourable reviews in *The Times,* 15 April, and *Spectator,* 18 May, 1901.

*standing so alone, so free from the finicking ornamentation
of which one wearies in China, has a dignity and a solemnity
which makes it worthy to be the central place of a nation's
worship . . . The mere existence of such a place, of such a
ceremony, is a convincing proof of the capacity of the
Chinese mind for true religious feeling, and throws into
horrid contrast the temples, Taoist or Buddhist, full of
tawdry ornaments and hideous idols.*

On August 23rd the missionaries set out as part of a convoy
of some eighty people. The road to T'ung-Chou was not very
good, *especially those places which were paved in Chinese fashion
with huge blocks of stone and had been allowed to go to ruin. A road of
this sort baffles description. Travellers may, and often do, exaggerate
the difficulties of journeys in China, but this road has and never can be
exaggerated.*

From T'ung-Chou, sacked and devastated by Russian troops,
the little party embarked on a grain boat: the two deaconesses
and their Chinese orphans slept in a matting shelter, whilst
Roland lay on the open deck with four 'Beloochi' guards. On this
vessel they drifted erratically downstream for four days to
Tientsin, shocked all the while by the unharvested countryside
around them:

*The foreigners seemed to be the only people in a land of
wealth. We saw also the signs of war only too frequently—
villages in flames, dead bodies floating down the river or
stranded on the banks. We shuddered to think of the deeds
committed by Christian troops and of the effect which they
must have upon the Chinese, and of the undying hatred
which was being planted with ever deeper and stronger roots
in their minds.*

In his reflections following the Siege, Roland's characteristic far-sightedness became apparent. Beholding a China *devastated, despoiled, ruined, depopulated, [which] must 'save face' or
perish,* he warned that *The danger to the West, the real Yellow Peril,
is not the Chinese alone . . . but the Chinese led by the Russians.* It

seemed clear to him that the *ill-advised philanthropy of America* was leading the West to *avoid present difficulties rather than overcome them . . . a consideration to make one alarmed for the future progress and peace of the world.*[4]

International politics, however, were the responsibility of others. Roland's concern was with the furtherance of the Christian faith. And by now his experiences in China were leading him to face several *fundamental questions in connexion with the propagation of the Church.*[5]

Almost as soon as the siege was over, Frances Scott, the Bishop's wife, was stricken with dysentery, and by doctor's orders was removed to Nagasaki, in Japan. Roland, with Deaconess Jessie, and two other missionaries, travelled to Nagasaki with the Scotts, and was with them there when Mrs. Scott died. Roland performed the last rites and conducted the burial service.[6]

The sadly diminished party then travelled on, across Canada and so at the beginning of December home at last to England, where Roland was assigned a dual role during his furlough—to act as chaplain to the Bishop and to be *the representative of a very much maligned mission.* For the Church had been reproached by people who alleged that many mere 'rice Christians' had renounced their shallow faith in the face of the Boxers' threats. Roland robustly challenged this view. In his opinion—

---

[4]See especially 'Of Some of the Conclusions which may be Drawn from the Siege of the Foreign Legations in Peking' and two preceeding articles in *The Cornhill Magazine*, No. 494 (February 1901).

[5]Report of an address to the Rotary Club of Nairobi: see the *East African Standard*, 23 June 1936.

[6]Roland dedicated to Mrs. Scott's memory his first book, *The Siege of the Peking Legations*, with these words:

IN PIAM MEMORIAM / DESIDERATISSIMAE DOMINAE
FRANCISCAE EMILIAE SCOTT / SPEI IN ADVERSIS
LAETITIAE IN PROSPERIS / CONSILII IN OMNIBUS
ADIVTRICIS CONSTANTISSIMAE.

When you have got a convert, you have got one, and he will stand by his faith, very often to the death . . . if you have Christians like that in a Church, that Church will grow. In Peking the Europeans were saved by the native Christians . . . Christian stands by Christian, racial instincts give way to religious . . . the conduct of the native Christians shows the power of this motive to make men stand by those from whom they have received spiritual benefits.

Moreover, he warned against the risk of racist views: *In dealing with the South African problem no-one fails to remember the necessity of using all possible means to overcome or weaken racial prejudices and ill-will. Surely, in dealing with the Chinese, this element in the problem cannot be disregarded.*[7]

The immediate purpose of Roland and his Bishop was to raise funds for the rehabilitation of all the mission stations that had been devastated during the Boxer uprising. But on several important occasions Roland took the opportunity to address far more fundamental issues. Thus in March 1901, as the principal speaker at an SPG bicentenary meeting for young people (which was chaired by the Archbishop of Canterbury himself) Roland expressed the opinion that—*Western teachers can never preach the whole Gospel to Eastern minds.*

In his view now, English-style theological colleges, such as the clergy school that he had himself been in charge of in Peking, were inappropriate: they *do not turn out apostles or evangelists, but deacons . . .*[8] As he was later to remark: *I saw that if the Church in North China was to have no clergy at all except such as could pass through my little theological school and then be financially supported, Churches could not multiply rapidly.*[9]

---

[7]Extracts from Roland's address to a Meeting for Youth, in Church House, Westminster, on March 9, 1901: *Report of the Bicentenary Celebration* (S.P.G.: 1903), pp. 139-141; see also 'Establishment of Indigenous Churches' (1927); and *The Cornhill Magazine, op.cit.*

[8]It may be noted that none of *these* opinions were included among the extracts selected from Roland's address for printing in the *Bicentenary Report*.

[9]'The Establishment of Indigenous Churches' (1927).

Moreover, he warned: *If the Church bears the mark 'Made in the West' too prominently stamped upon her, many will turn away from her who would not turn away from Christ . . . Constant guidance and supervision by Europeans may outwit its own purpose.* Already he saw the danger that—not only in China: *Opposition to Western civilization will be opposition to 'the white man's Gospel' . . . Western civilization is not a good revelation of Christ and the Gospel.*[10]

He accepted that possibly a distinction needed to be made between Africans with *no native tradition of formulated worship*, and Chinese or Indians with long established religious civilizations. He also wondered whether:

> *When many different races and tongues meet in one spot, as e.g. in India or in South Africa, is it desirable to have Bishops for different languages, Assistant Bishops?*

Roland was fiercely critical of the sort of possessiveness at that time being expressed by some of the great missionary societies in words such as these:

> *It would be neither right nor wise to interfere with the unity of the Church by setting up an imperium in imperio; but on the other hand it is reasonable that the C.M.S.'s property, such as mission churches, parsonages, school houses, etc, should only be transferred to the independent Churches and its funds granted, with some security for their just and proper use and application.*[11]

This would be no 'independent Church', protested Roland: *Liberty which is not liberty to err is not liberty. There is no possibility of virtue without a possibility of vice. Orthodoxy based on ignorant acceptance of authority or upon fearful obedience to rules is not orthodoxy; it is not a 'doxy' at all . . . It is a house built upon sand.*[12]

---

[10]*Le Zoute—a Critical Review* (World Dominion Press: 1927), pp. 19, 34.

[11]Church Missionary Society, *Memorandum, §21* (April 1901), p. 251.

[12]From handwritten notes on a talk 'to a clerical society in E. London - c.1901'.

Roland acknowledged that a policy such as he was advocating—namely, to hand over full responsibility to the indigenous Christians within the shortest possible time—must seem fraught with risk. But he met this challenge head-on:

> *What is to ensure orthodoxy? Nothing: no power can ensure orthodoxy but the power of the Holy Spirit.*

At a conference in Manchester nearly two years later, Roland was to give an address on this same topic: *'The Work of the Missionary in Preparing the Way for Independent Native Churches'—because I believe that this is the greatest and most important problem which the Church in the Mission field is now called upon to face.* By that time he had himself had an opportunity to put some of his ideas into practice. Roland reiterated that—*The first work of the missionary should be to train his converts in real independence.* In order to fulfil this responsibility, he put forward three key principles:

i) *to teach the native converts to recognize their responsibility as members of the Church . . . never to do for the natives anything that they could do for themselves . . .*

ii) *to avoid the introduction of any foreign element unless it is absolutely essential . . .* [otherwise] *the books, the vestments, the ornaments, the design of the building, all come from a foreign land . . . the Church is the foreigners' Church.*

iii) *to be always retiring from the people, to prepare the way for final retirement . . . To become indispensable to the people is really to fail . . .* [Rather the missionary should] *patiently watch while the Holy Spirit transforms strange forms of life into Christian forms of life unlike our own.*[13]

In a strong letter to The Guardian in July 1902, writing under his Chinese pseudonym 'Lien', he pointed out the impossibility of ever supplying the need of men for missions of the orthodox type, and argued that the unceasing appeal for men was based

---

[13]Federation of Junior Church Missionary Associates, *Report of 19th Conference of Delegates* (Manchester: November 1903).

61

on false premises: *a false view of our missionary purpose . . . the idea that the missions of the Church are to be little copies of the Church of England at home . . . All the ministers of the new Churches must be educated in a long and tedious course of Western controversy . . .* This letter provoked one hearty endorsement in the form of a letter three weeks later from one 'W.C.R.', in which, interestingly, occur two phrases which Roland was later to make his own—*the methods of St. Paul* and the *spontaneous expansion* of the Church.

One fascinated listener to this unorthodox missionary had been active on behalf of the North China Mission for even longer than Roland himself. Miss Mary Beatrice Tarleton (1863 - 1960) had by this time lost both her parents. She was the elder of the two younger sisters of Alfred Henry Tarleton of Breakspears, near Uxbridge. She does not seem to have had any very particular connection with China. But she had long been a friend of Jessie Ransome, who first aroused her interest in the Mission, and who actually introduced her to Roland.

Another very indirect connection with China was that Beatrice's father, Admiral Sir (John) Walter Tarleton KCB (1811-80), had owed his advancement in the Royal Navy partly to his service on the China station early in his career. When Captain Tarleton's ship arrived off the Isle of Wight on her return home to England one morning after several years' service in the Far East, he received a signal to say that Queen Victoria was in residence at Osborne House. He ordered his weary, but well trained, ship's company to dress ship, and they had HMS *Euryalus* looking so smart, as she came sailing by, that she was noticed by the Queen from the terrace. *That is a very smart ship,* remarked Her Majesty, *Who is her commander?—Captain Tarleton,* she was told. *Never heard of him!* said she, and then after a moment's reflection: *Why have I not heard of him?*

When it was explained to the Queen that Tarleton had been away, and that this vessel had sailed in that very morning from China, after spending no less than seven years on the Pacific Station, she was even more impressed by its smartness: so she required the captain to be summoned to audience. Now it so happened that all the senior naval captains were at that time competing for the honour of taking to sea the Queen's second son, Prince Alfred, but she had found herself unable to choose among them. She immediately took a liking to the bluff Captain Tarleton, with his very 'Victorian' beard and sideburns, and she made a snap decision, there and then, to entrust him with taking the Prince to sea in *Euryalus* as a naval cadet.[14]

Sir Walter later became an aide-de-camp to the Queen, a Lord Commissioner of the Admiralty (1871-74), and Admiral Superintendent of Naval Reserves (1874-77). His household was run on as disciplinarian lines as his ship. Grannie recalled, for instance, that she was not allowed downstairs in any circumstances after her supper-time: so, even on one occasion when Jenny Lind came to sing before dinner, Beatrice and Edith might only listen from the top of the stairs.

Prince Alfred always retained great personal affection for his first commander. He stood godfather to the Tarletons' eldest son, to whom they gave the name Alfred after him, and who served in the Prince's ship when he in turn was a naval cadet. The Prince often used to come to the Tarletons' London home to consult the old man, when Beatrice was still a girl. She used to recall how—shockingly—the indecorous prince was in the habit of running upstairs to Sir Walter's room, two steps at a time. On one occasion, when the butler divulged to the waiting cab driver the identity of his royal fare, Grannie was delighted to see the cabbie solemnly take out a pair of white gloves and put them on.

In another sartorial tale, Grannie used to recount to us how her father requested his coxwain to make sailor suits for herself and her elder brother. A few days' afterwards, when the children were playing in St. James's Park, a resplendent footman

---

[14]The Prince's illustrated log-book is preserved in the Royal Library at Windsor Castle; its decorative title-page reads: *Log of the Proceedings of H.M.S. "Euryalus" 51 commanded by Capt J W Tarleton CB: kept by Alfred, N.C. commencing 31st of August, 1858. Ending February 28th 1860* (Royal Collection, Windsor Royal Library, 1B 5A). Prince Alfred later became Duke of Edinburgh, and later still Duke of Saxe-Coburg and Gotha.

summoned them and their nanny to a passing brougham, in which Queen Victoria herself was taking the air. She asked their names, and remarked: *I know your father well. Pray tell him that I like your attire.* A day or two later the coxwain was instructed to produce similar garments for two of the royal grandchildren—and a fashion was set that swept through the western world for several decades!

Beatrice and her sister Edith thus lived on the fringes of court society. As children they were sometimes invited to the palace to play with the royal children, and later the two of them were once or twice invited to royal dances. They both attended the first ball at Buckingham Palace at which electric lighting was used. The occasion turned out to be a disaster, for every lady's face had been made up to appear in gas or candlelight: and so they one and all looked hideous in the unaccustomed glare!

The two girls could have become ladies-in-waiting: but their father died while they were still teenagers, and their mother soon afterwards. Their elder brother and other members of the family considered that Queen Victoria's court was no place for unaccompanied young gentlewomen. They were only permitted to attend concerts or the opera by going up to the gallery, as diligent students with their music scores, rather than socializing in the main part of the theatre. Their only really helpful chaperone was one 'Cousin Bessie', who took them on trips to Italy and elsewhere with her own two daughters.[15]

The two young ladies, especially the strong-willed Beatrice, grew tired of their elder relatives' continual criticism. So they decided to move out into their own home, where they applied themselves to 'good works'—in particular for the North China Mission Association. By 1896 Beatrice was on the Association's central committee, and she had become Honorary Secretary and

---

[15]'Cousin Bessie' Wilbraham was mother-in-law of Francis Turner Palgrave, the compiler of the well-known anthology, *The Golden Treasury*. He was to stand as one of the godfathers of Beatrice's daughter, Priscilla.

Treasurer of its Peking Medical Mission. Her devoted sister, Edith, was also an active supporter and committee member.

In 1901's autumn number of the Mission journal, The Land of Sinim, Bishop Scott was pleased to make an announcement in his quarterly letter:

> *Mr. Allen, too, is engaged to be married to a very staunch and warm friend of the North China Mission, Miss Tarleton, who is well known to many of you, and who has done very valuable service for many years in connection with the Medical Mission.*

CHAPTER VI

Marriage and Yung-Ch'ing

The Misses Tarleton
at Home
Wednesday, October 16th
4 to 6 o'clock.

The Marriage of
the Rev. Roland Allen
and Miss Mary Beatrice Tarleton
will take place at
St. Peter's Church Eaton Square
on Thursday, October 17th
at 8 a.m.

'Beatrice and her sister Edith
themselves made all the arrangements'

Beatrice Tarleton was nearing forty years of age—over five
years older than the magnetic missionary—but their forceful

and independent personalities were drawn together, and they quickly got married, even though several of my grandmother's relatives felt that Beatrice was 'marrying beneath her'.

Grannie was indeed comparatively blue-blooded. Her mother was Finetta, daughter and co-heir of the 4th Hon. Baron Dimsdale; whilst her father, Sir Walter, traced ancestry to Edward III's son, John of Gaunt. The family trees include several notable personalities, among them the only English Pope, Nicholas Breakspear (Adrian IV, d.1159), who crowned the Emperor Frederick Barbarossa; and England's last court jester, Richard Tarlton (d.1588), who was one of the original company of Queen's Players and their chief comedian. He was Queen Elizabeth's favourite clown, particularly renowned for impromptu doggerel verses. After his death several volumes of *Tarlton's Jests* were published, although many of the witticisms attributed to him are much older. He was said to have been the inspiration for Hamlet's Yorick.

Beatrice's great-grandfather was a Quaker physician. Dr. Thomas Dimsdale, FRS, MP (1712-1800), the 1st Hon. Baron Dimsdale, was an early practitioner of the Suttonian technique of inoculation for smallpox. In 1768 he was invited to Saint Petersburg to vaccinate the Empress Catherine of Russia and her family. For this service both he and his son were created Barons of Russia; they returned to St. Petersburg in 1781 to vaccinate Catherine's grandchildren.

On the other side of the family Beatrice had a great-uncle, Sir Banastre Tarleton, Bart., GCB, MP (1754-1833), lamentably described in one biographical dictionary as: *Only successful British commander in American War of Independence; noted for his cruelty to prisoners.* As the commander of 'Tarleton's Green Horse' in the British Legion, Banastre was prominent in numerous fiery engagements, from Bigging Bridge and the capture of Charleston in 1780 to the siege of Gloucester eighteen months' later. One account says of him that *He was a born cavalry leader, with great dash, and as such was unequalled in his time.* From 1790 for more than twenty years he was Member of Parliament for Liverpool;

and he finished his career as Governor of Berwick-on-Tweed. He was a member of the notorious 'Hell Fire Club' and alleged to have been the model for Baroness Orczy's *Scarlet Pimpernel*. A splendid portrait by Sir Joshua Reynolds depicts him in action at the battle of Guilford Courthouse (where he lost two fingers of his right hand); the picture now hangs in London's National Gallery, having been left to the nation by Beatrice's brother Alfred in lieu of death duties.

Owing to the disapproval of their brother and other relatives, Beatrice and her sister Edith themselves made all the arrangements both for the wedding ceremony and for the reception.[1] Bishop Scott was very anxious to get back to China; by arranging for the wedding to be at 8 o'clock in the morning, with the reception at the Tarleton sisters' London home the night before, it was made possible for both him and the Deaconess Jessie to participate, and still get to Euston in time to catch their train to Liverpool, whence the S.S. *Pretoria* was about to depart. And so the Bishop could write in his next quarterly letter:

> *Many of our friends . . . were able to meet at St. Peter's, Eaton Square, and receive the Holy Communion together on the morning of October 17, when Mr. Allen and Miss Tarleton were married. It was a great pleasure to me to perform the marriage rite.*[2]

The celebrant was Granfer's 'dear Father in God', Pusey's Librarian, the Revd Dr. F.E. Brightman; and the address was given by another Oxford scholar—namely Willoughby, Roland's brother from Exeter College.

The happy couple had a very short honeymoon, with one night at an hotel in Burford in Oxfordshire, and the rest of a week at Crickhowell in Wales. Then Roland continued his work in

---

[1]As a token of gratitude to Edith for helping to arrange the wedding, Roland gave to his new sister-in-law a copy of John Bunyan's *Pilgrim's Progress*, sumptuously bound in dark purple velvet with silver clasps.

[2]*The Land of Sinim*, Vol.X/1 (January 1902), p. 5.

England for a further year. At the end of 1902, after his very extended furlough—*spent in much successful labour for the Mission, preaching and lecturing in every direction*—the recently married couple set sail together in S.S.*Kiaoutchou*; and in December they settled down at the mission station in Yung Ch'ing. It was there that Roland's fellow clergy, Mr. Norman and Mr. Robinson, had both been murdered by the Boxers early in June 1900, just before the siege of the legations began in Peking itself. By this time their old friend Deaconess Jessie Ransome was there too, in charge of women's work—although, sadly, only for a short time: for in 1905 she was to die of a sudden and acute attack of dysentery (and *not*, as some people later suggested, of a broken heart after Roland's marriage to another!).

Only three months after the Allens' arrival in Yung Ch'ing, in spite of Beatrice's advanced age, The Land of Sinim was able to *have great pleasure in announcing that Mrs. Allen has given birth to a little girl . . . both doing very well indeed.*[3] Deaconess Jessie and Bishop Scott stood godparents to the baby Priscilla, who was born on 15th March. However, only a month or two later, the Bishop had to report in his quarterly letter that *Mr. Allen has had a very sharp attack of fever (? malarial) and he and Mrs. Allen and their little girl have been spending two or three weeks at St. Hilary's to recruit.* Sadly, this convalescence was not enough, and the editor of The Land of Sinim had to report in the same number of the journal that:

> We very much regret to know that the Doctors have ordered
> Mr. Allen to leave China, where his work at Yung-Ch'ing
> was giving such promise. He and Mrs. Allen are now on
> their way home.[4]

Roland's erstwhile siege companion, the Revd. Frank L. Norris, was very distressed: in a letter to Beatrice he remarked

---

[3]Vol.XI/2 (April 1903), p. 23: summary biographies of both Priscilla and her brother are given at Appendix 1.

[4]Vol.XI/3 (July 1903), pp. 4 & 7.

that: *No-one we have ever had in the Mission can do what he has done, or take his place.*

Although his poor health had allowed him to stay in China for so very few more months, Roland—

> *did great things for Yung-Ch'ing. Mr. Allen's keen enthusiasm to some extent infected the Christians, and the results were immediately apparent in several directions . . . a real revival of personal religion . . . a beginning in the direction of self-government . . . and an effort to take up work at Ch'i-Chou started by the Rev. Norman.*[5]

Roland's initiatives, it should be noted, were fully backed by most of the other members of the Mission: *The Bishop is heartily in sympathy with me,* he remarks in his account of the experiments. At a clergy meeting in Peking as early as the New Year's Day of 1902, resolutions had been passed to try to make the native Church much more self-sufficient, on lines similar to those advocated in 1885 by the Presbyterian missionary, Dr. Nevius, in articles in The Chinese Recorder, and put into practice by him in Korea five years later.[6]

This is how the challenge had been put by Frank Norris:

> *Are we to respond to the call so splendidly set forth by the Bishop of Uganda at the Church Congress . . . to break away from our old traditions of 'nursing' the native church, and rather to aim, at all costs, at helping it to be self-extending, self-supporting, and self-governing?*[7]

Roland's assignment to Yung-Ch'ing allowed him to try to put into effect some of the missionary principles he and his comrades had been advocating: *I urged upon my evangelists that*

---

[5]Norris, *op. cit.*

[6]Note an article on the 'Nevius Method', and a somewhat critical rejoinder by Roland, in *World Dominion* (July 1930).

[7]*The Land of Sinim*, Vol. X/2 (April 1902), pp. 14-15, 34. In later years Roland, too, was to refer to Bishop Tucker's ideas, but to suggest that they did not go far enough: see *The Spontaneous Expansion of the Church*, pp. 35ff.

their business was not to induce people to accept a book or a system as a whole, but to understand the principles. From the very first there is a great deal that new converts can do for themselves . . . [and consequently] They will be healthy; they will grow.[8]

A scarcely disguised account of Roland's experiment was to be set out by him nearly ten years' later in the Epilogue to his first seminal publication, *Missionary Methods: St. Paul's or Ours?*—

He began by approaching his Bishop with a request that the usual grant given for the upkeep of his mission station might be withdrawn. He desired that his own salary and the salaries of his three native catechists might be paid them, but no more.

In this very densely populated area—*a plain covered with trees, crops, villages and life,* where it was *quite impossible to get out of sight of two or three villages,* Roland started to oversee the work of three of his former pupils: Shih Hung Chang, who had arrived at Peking Clergy Training School with his family as a refugee from the Boxers after the murder of Mr. Brooks at the end of 1899, and had been got safely away to Tientsin before the Siege; and Lei Yü Chün and Wang Shu T'ien, whose escape from Peking in 1900 had occasioned so much anxiety for Roland and Norris.[9] All three of these were now catechists based in "Church-rooms" either in Yung-Ch'ing or near by, at Han-ko-Chuang; and in Roland's 'parish' there was also a Christian village being developed at Shih Min Chuang, on land that had been confiscated from local Boxer leaders by the Chinese authorities.

In all these places Roland persuaded the local Christians to elect church councils, under the leadership of church wardens—one of them appointed by the congregation, and only one by the foreign missionaries; he then arranged for these councils to send representatives to a 'common council', to which he

---

[8]Letter — signed under the pseudonym 'Lien' — 'The Unceasing Appeal for Men for Foreign Missions,' *The Guardian,* 23 July 1902, p. 1075.

[9]See *The Siege of the Peking Legations,* pp. 46, 49 and 60ff.

handed over almost all the responsibility for finance, for missionary evangelism, and for church government and discipline. In an article in the Mission's journal about his work, Roland emphasizes over and over again his determination to get away from traditional missionary paternalism:

> *e.g. at Han-Ko-Chuang the Christians wanted to found a small school. They asked me to do it. I refused. Then they tried to make a compromise by asking me to find the teacher. I refused again. I said that the school must be their school and that they must manage it, but that I would give a small subscription. In the event they did open a school, to which the Mission gave a grant of £1.1s. a year.*

In *Missionary Methods* Roland recounts how discipline was enforced, not by the missionaries but by the indigenous Church— even when the methods flew in the face of their own cultural predispositions. When one of the catechists heard from Roland how he thought a penitent should be called upon to act in one very serious case, he protested incredulously: *'Such a thing has never been done since the world began. Whatever [the offender] may do, he will not do that.'* Yet he did, reports Roland, *It is one thing to be excommunicated by a foreign bishop, it is quite another to be excommunicated by one's neighbours.*

At Ch'i-Chou, a village where the Revd. H.V. Norman had begun work before his murder, we can see Roland already beginning to put into practice the very methods of St. Paul:

> *I sent at first Shih Hung Chang and Wang Shu T'ien [the appropriately christened 'Timothy'] to prospect, and they brought back such a glowing report that I soon after sent Wang Shu T'ien and an old Christian named Hsü Tien Kuei, on a six weeks' visit. They preached to over 550 people, and left in one village a little community of seven hearers pledged to meet not less than once a week. They first recite an abbreviated creed, taught them by Wang Shu T'ien (practically the explanation of the creed from the Church Catechism), then they read a portion of the gospels, and then they offer*

prayer to the best of their ability. They are to meet in the house of one of their number, who has set aside a room for the purpose, and they receive no support of any kind from foreign funds. I sincerely hope that this may grow into a self-governing, self-supporting church in these parts. All that is needed is frequent visitation for further instruction. I should wish to see Shu T'ien sent out often on these missionary tours, for which he is eminently fitted.[10]

Roland's ambition was to withdraw quickly from direct involvement at Yung-Ch'ing and in its neighbourhood, and to go off and work in other villages:

Personally I can see at present no reason why it should be necessary to keep a foreigner here more than a year or two longer, and even now I think the continued presence of a foreigner rather a disadvantage than otherwise.[11]

And in less than six months one of the catechists came into Roland's house with a question: *Do you know what you are doing, sir?*—Yes, replied Roland, *I think that I know; but I should like to know what you think I am doing.*—Well, sir, if you go on like this you will found a native Church.

Tragically—as it seemed to him and Beatrice, and to their North China Mission—Roland's precarious health now deteriorated; and so he was invalided home after no more than nine months back in China: *we can scarcely overestimate the disappointment to them and the great loss to the people of Yung-Ch'ing by their withdrawal.*[12] Wang Shu T'ien gave him as a farewell present a fine wash landscape painting by himself, with a poetic inscription.

Roland quickly resumed activity in England on behalf of the mission, *which will be all the more valuable because of this brief space*

---

[10]*The Land of Sinim,* Vol.XI/4 (October 1903), pp. 18, 20.

[11]*The Anglican Mission at Yung Ch'ing, North China,* (leaflet dated February 20th, 1903).

[12]*The Land of Sinim,* Vol.XI/4 (October 1903), Editorial, p.5.

of work and experience in Yung-Ch'ing; and Beatrice also threw herself back into work, as Secretary of the St. Faith's Associates, supporting the Deaconesses' work among Chinese women.

As he recovered his health, Roland begged to be allowed to resume his work in North China: but the Society was convinced that this would be too much of a risk. This decision made him very unhappy, believing in his depression that people did not *want* him in China any more. However, he consented instead to become an ordinary vicar in an English parish; and so his Oxford College (St. John's) arranged to prefer him to one of their numerous benefices—the rural Buckinghamshire parish of Chalfont St. Peter.

He was somewhat irritated by the reactions of many acquaintances to this development, which was in stark contrast to *the general impression that a man who goes to China as a missionary is nothing more than a harmless lunatic:*

> *If an able-bodied young man in England accepts a tiny country living with absolutely no scope for his energies and abilities, his friends inundate him with letters of congratulation; but if a man intimates that he is going out as a missionary to a life and work that makes a demand upon all of a whole man, he is considered beside himself.*[13]

However, Roland was destined to put all this disappointment to very fruitful use:

> *I was ill, and came home for two years, and begun to study the methods of the Apostle St.Paul. From that day forward I began to see light.*[14]

---

[13]Vol.XII/3 (July 1904), p. 19.
[14]*Church Missionary Review*, June 1927.

CHAPTER VII

The End of the Beginning

**'Their three years at Chalfont St. Peter
were the happiest of Grannie's life'**

Soon after their arrival at Chalfont St. Peter, at the age of forty-one, Beatrice bore Roland a second child.[1] This little boy (my father) was born on November 14th, 1904, in the neighbouring village of Chalfont Saint Giles. He was christened John—or rather 'Iohn', as Granfer somewhat inexplicably entered the

---

[1]See summary biography, Appendix 1[B].

name in the baptismal register, 'in accordance with ancient custom'.

Roland and Beatrice quickly settled into the life of a country vicarage, and were very happy and active. Both kept up some of their work for the North China Mission. And from time to time they were able to leave the children in the care of a nanny, or Beatrice's sister Edith (now herself married), and to take holidays in Europe. In one year they appear from Roland's photographs to have spent a holiday in Portugal. And in April and May of 1907 they spent four weeks touring Switzerland, making a very thorough collection of postcards of all the places they visited. Roland in particular, however, seems to have been much more interested in the way of life and customs of the people they met than in architecture and scenery. For him one of the greatest delights was to relish examples of cross-cultural understanding and misunderstanding—such as the English version of a notice outside the hospitable premises of some monks in the Alps:

> *The Brothers of the Misericord*
> *harbour every kind of disease*
> *and have no respect for religion.*

Their three years at Chalfont St. Peter were the happiest of Grannie's life, so she was very distressed, although loyally supportive, when on November 25th, 1907, Roland addressed a long circular letter to all his parishioners, in which he publicly and pugnaciously resigned (see Appendix 2). He did this because he found himself unable conscientiously to carry out his legal duty, as a priest in the established Church of England, to perform solemn religious ceremonies even for undeserving persons who *habitually neglect their religious duties, or openly deny the truth of the Creeds, or by the immorality of their lives openly defy the laws of God.*[2]

---

[2]This was an early example of Roland's thinking being ahead of his time. The problem faced by clergy, required by law to baptize children of unbelievers, was a matter for lively debate in the Church of England's General Synod in 1991.

The Church of England, Roland protested, as the established church of the nation, demanded *the acquiescence of a priest in a practice which he cannot justify*, as regards baptisms, marriages and burial services. After all his experience in the mission field, Roland could not accept that the Church should be used as no more than a convenient and fashionable social service. Although not mentioned in the resignation letter, the particular incident that crystallized his resolve was when he was called upon to conduct in church the burial service for a suicide—for an unbelieving member of an eminent local family (that is to say, a wealthy and influential parishioner, not a poor person, whose family might have supposed that the vicar was snobbishly discriminating against them).

As Roland's letter of resignation makes clear, the occasion of it was by no means the first time that he had felt disturbed by custom and the law. He had frequently made his opinions very clear to his parishioners *to the point of seriously annoying some of you*. On one memorable occasion, a wealthy bridegroom, who was a resident in the parish but a notorious unbeliever, pointed out to Roland that, even as incumbent parish priest, he could not lawfully prevent his wedding being celebrated in the parish church of Chalfont St. Peter provided that another priest could be found, who was willing to perform the ceremony. Roland responded cheerfully: *Yes, that is perfectly true. And no more can you lawfully prevent me, as the incumbent parish priest, from tolling the funeral bell throughout the proceedings* . . .

Numerous newspapers, both national and regional, gave prominence to his 'remarkable statement', and quoted extensively from it. But most of them were cautious in their editorial comment, confining themselves on the whole to such laudatory headlines as 'A Manly Vicar', 'Vicar's Sacrifice', 'Good Man Weary'.[3]

---

[3]See the *Daily Telegraph* (13.12.1907), *Cooperative Times* (21.12.1907), *Daily Chronicle* (15.12.1907), *Liverpool Evening Express* (16.12.1907), and *News of the World* (15.12.1907).

The religious press was a little more forthright: *It is refreshing to read of such moral courage and frankness;Missionaries are unable to acclimatize themselves with what seems to others the nominal Christianity, but is in reality the paganism, of the careless and indifferent among us ... Mr. Allen has shown by his sacrifice that he is prepared to act on his convictions.*[4]

Not a few Church of England clergy sympathized with his bold action in resigning, as can be seen from contemporary correspondence in The Guardian and The Church Times in which Roland's conscientious protest was debated. However, even the most outspoken among them felt obliged to remain anonymous, unless they had already retired. Thus 'An East Anglian Rector,' with long experience in both urban and rural parishes, remarked that *the present method of administering Baptism in the Church of England is a scandal to religion, a disgrace to the Church, a degradation of the Sacrament ...* And a 'Winchester Diocesan Missioner' commented that *Holy Baptism is administered with a carelessness which would astonish the Christians of Central Africa, and which must make the angels weep ...*

But, as Roland points out, these parochial clergy, although *they do not even attempt to defend themselves* against his reproach, were one and all *bound by fetters of law and custom and habit and poverty ... It is true that they are bound by law to do these things, but law cannot justify impiety, and it is impiety to take God's Holy Name in vain.*

Roland made it very clear that no-one should suppose him to be forsaking the Church:

> *That is quite a mistake ... I am protesting against a misuse of her rites; to her principles I am profoundly attached. I have no quarrel with my Bishop, or with my Church ... What I think is needed is ... a determined effort to secure a greater freedom to exercise a proper discipline.*[5]

---

[4]*The Baptist* (19.12.1907); and *Church of Ireland Gazette* (20.12.1907)
[5]See *The Guardian* (5.2.1908), *Church Times* (27.12 and 20.12.1907), and *Tribune* (20 December, following up an article of 12 December 1907).

On the eve of his departure from the parish, more than two hundred of his congregation—*thoroughly representative of every phase of religious thought in the parish* in the words of a local newspaper—subscribed to an illuminated address, which was presented to him. Accompanying the address was an elegant tea-service of sterling silver, the teapot bearing the inscription *To the Revd. Roland Allen from Parishioners of Chalfont St. Peter, Christmas 1907.* To this day this silver service still bears eloquent testimony that many of his flock were as sad to lose him after such a brief incumbency as he and Grannie were to go.

In voicing his thanks, Roland gave expression to another of his concerns, in which he was once more somewhat ahead of his time—the potential role of the *laity* in the life of the Church. He remarked that he

> *felt more than strengthened in his opinion that the Church would go forward more and more in this country as the laity cooperated more and more in the work of the Church, as they realised more and more that the work of the Church was not the work of the individual priest, but it was the church of the laity, and not merely the church of the clergy.*

Notwithstanding his popularity, however, the law for the established Church was such that, as Roland had explained to his parishioners, *I cannot act as I am determined to act, and yet hold any benefice in England.* Beatrice made an appeal to Bishop Scott in China for help, but he had to telegraph back that in the circumstances there was nothing more that he could do for them.

Roland's daughter Priscilla was in later life occasionally somewhat caustic about his resignation, saying he was able to do it only because he could live on his wife's money: she felt that he was selfishly inclined to subordinate the happiness of his wife and family to his perceived mission. This unswerving dedication to his mission is unquestionable, although it is perhaps harsh to describe it as selfish, or—in retrospect—to agree with Priscilla that it was 'very sad' that he was 'banished from active life'. On the contrary, at least one commentator has remarked that *those who are interested in Allen will believe that his resignation from the parish was really the beginning of his ministry, and not the end of it!* [6]

Beatrice herself was completely dedicated to her husband's welfare and his mission. She never appears to have questioned his decisions, and applied herself to helping him in any and every possible way, principally by managing the household and by acting as his amanuensis whenever he had need. She had no intellectual pretensions, and was very reluctant, after his death, to comment on his work in any way, even within the family. In a letter she wrote to me in 1954, in reply to a question of mine about 'voluntary clergy', she concluded: *My dear, I hesitate to write as I have, as - tho' I wrote most of his books in his dictation, I never wrote anything off my own without him.*

As regards money, Roland took issue fiercely with any imputations that he was mercenary. One of his nephews recalls him as a visiting preacher many years later, addressing a congregation to this effect: *I am tired of being told that I preach the Gospel because I am paid to, not because I believe it myself. If you hear me preach the Gospel again, invited by your next Vicar, I shall not be paid.* His daughter remarked that *my father had no use for money except, like St. Paul, for traveling.* [7]

On this topic his son Iohn once wrote about Roland:

> So few of us practise what we preach that we find it hard to believe that anyone does. To take an example that he would call trivial, but most of us would not—few of us believe that anybody can be indifferent to money unless he has a lot of it. My father was genuinely indifferent, and therefore gave the impression that he was rich . . . [8]

---

[6]The Revd. H. Boone Porter, *private communication.*

[7]'Roland Allen: a Prophet for this Age', *The Living Church,* 192/16 (April 20, 1986), p. 11.

[8]Letter to Sir Kenneth Grubb, 7th January 1967.

What was more, Roland was soon to be advocating that *we need today a kind of counter-poverty in the clergy; not the poverty which says, I will abandon all other means of livelihood in order to minister to my fellows; but the kind of poverty which says, I will not receive anything from my fellows for ministering to them in spiritual things.*[9]

Deprived of his livelihood, Roland devoted some of his time to deputation work for overseas missions, and occasionally did relief duty for fellow clergy during sickness. Otherwise he lived in some seclusion with his little family, first on Primrose Hill in north London and later in a small house in the Hertfordshire village of Harpenden, close to Beatrice's brother's home at Breakspears. There he devoted himself more and more to thinking and to writing.

Roland and Beatrice brought up their two children in a way that was far from orthodox, to the extent of being eccentric. Neither of them had had much experience of young children, so from a very early age they tended to treat them as adults. It was taken for granted that both children would share the parents' interests. Both of them learned to play chess at an early age. Moreover, outdoor recreation was much more likely to be a cycle ride to explore medieval country churches, than participation in any active games.

The strict naval discipline of Grannie's childhood was reflected in her own children's upbringing. The young brother and sister were required to behave with adult patience and decorum, not to say stoicism. Every plateful of food had to be cleared of its contents, however disagreeable, so that to the end of his days my father felt embarrassed to set aside anything that had been served to him, and was in some distress, in Muslim countries, to remember that to clear one's plate implies that the host has not offered enough!

---

[9]'The Case for Voluntary Clergy: an Anglican Problem', *The Interpreter*, July 1922, p. 314ff.

One of their younger cousins, Dick Allen, recalled that he *used to find his Aunt B rather formidable. Her talents seemed to him to be intellectual rather than domestic. For example, she once fed him raw porridge oats under the impression that these were breakfast cereals.* Dick's elder brother, Derick, also recalls this episode, but heartily endorses his brother's subsequent remark that both Roland and Beatrice *were, indeed, most kindly and generous people.*

However, this severely regimented upbringing may well, in fact, have saved my father's life: at the age of five or six he was bowling a hoop downstairs, when he lost his balance and fell heavily, so that the hoop-stick was rammed into his face, breaking bones around the ear. The surgeon was at a loss to know what to do: *He is too shocked to survive an anaesthetic. But while I am operating the pain will be acute; and if he moves even a very little, a splinter of bone may well penetrate his brain and kill him. If I tell him to lie still,* said Beatrice, *he will do so.* And so it proved.

Much later on, my mother would recall staying with her husband's parents, in order to visit her sister, who was in a nearby hospital, dangerously ill. When Winkie wanted to visit her sister every day, Beatrice thought her daughter-in-law to be making a most unnecessary fuss, and on one occasion rebuked her, saying: *We do not cry in this house.* Beatrice's niece Finetta recalls:

> *Crying was frowned upon in my childhood. The first things I learnt when I went to school at the age of 4 were that two things were socially unacceptable: (a) to cry for any reason whatsoever, & (b) to be seen being wheeled in a pram or push-chair.*

Priscilla's and Iohn's elderly and intellectual parents tended to keep themselves and their children aloof from most neighbours. And they seem to have assumed that their offspring would share their contempt for pointless athleticism. The two children's principal playfellows, for much of their youth, were Watkin and Mary Wynn-Williams, the son and daughter of another rather elderly and eccentrically intellectual couple. They were also very fond of their cousins, Tom and Finetta Brandreth: but they lived in Weybridge, many miles' cycle ride away from any of the Allen homes. Their mother Edith (Beatrice's younger sister) had married a naval officer late in 1903.

It would be a mistake to suppose that the Allens were reclusive on account of social gentility. I recall my mother once commenting ruefully:

> *The Allens simply didn't understand snobbery. We Brookes were snobs—'landed gentry', you know—but Grannie was quite unselfconsciously a true aristocrat, whilst Granfer simply didn't understand what 'class' was all about. Whether duke or dustman, he was conscious only that they had souls to save . . .*

Roland was well aware of the phenomenon, however: years later, during his visit to Assam, he identified three men, whom he thought admirably fitted for service as 'voluntary clergy'. *But I am afraid that the Bishop will want an 'educated gentleman' and will jib at ordaining 3 foremen of the lower middle class . . .*

Meanwhile Roland was busy reading (notably the New Testament studies by Adolf von Harnack and Professor W.M. Ramsay), and beginning to write. His first extended essay in missionary theology—a pamphlet entitled *Foundation Principles of Foreign Missions*—seems to have been completed in about 1910. It was printed by Richard Clay & Sons in Suffolk, but does not appear to have been published. In it we already see what Boer describes as *'the high and lofty significance which Allen ascribed to the Holy Spirit'*: (see next chapter). *We are missionaries of the Gospel, not of the law,* he writes, *we administer the Spirit, not the letter.*

In that same year, 1910, a great World Missionary Conference was held in Edinburgh. This gathering has been described somewhere as 'the apotheosis of missionary triumphalism'. Although the rapporteur, W.H.T. Gairdner, and his wife were later to become close friends of the Allens, the conference epitomized all Roland's worst misgivings about the current attitudes of western missionaries—their conscious and unconscious paternalism, their clericalism, their colonialism. So, as a former colleague has put it: *Allen turned back to the Christian Book of Instructions.*[10]

At the end of that year Roland and Beatrice contrived to travel out to India together for a couple of months. They went to Delhi, Calcutta and Madras, and Roland was invited to preach in these and several smaller places: letters to their two children are preserved, from Barisal in the Ganges delta, and from Ramnad, far to the south near the great temples of Madurai. They undertook a 30-mile bicycle ride to Murhu mission station in Ranchi, near Chota Nagpur, where they attended the laying of the foundation stone of a hospital and school, and spent Christmas in the bungalow of a Dr. and Mrs. Kennedy.

During this tour, Roland was able to talk to many people active in mission work in India, among them notably Vedanayakam Samuel Azariah, later to become Bishop of Dornakal; and probably Bishop Henry Whitehead of Madras.[11] These discussions helped to reinforce his growing convictions, and to give them a wider base than his experiences in the single mission field of China.

And so, in February 1912, with a laudatory preface by Bishop Whitehead, there appeared the seminal book on which Roland's reputation during his lifetime was principally to be founded—the wryly entitled *Missionary Methods: St. Paul's or Ours?* The book is divided into five parts, each meticulously argued. In the first part Roland examines the environment in which St.Paul actually worked. In the second he reviews the way in which the Apostle presented the Gospel. The third part looks at his training of converts. The fourth discusses his handling

---

[10]Francesca French, *Thomas Cochrane* (Hodder & Stoughton: 1956), p. 100.

[11]A year or two later, Bishop Whitehead was to write to Roland, thanking him warmly for coming to the defence of Azariah's appointment as Bishop — an appointment (of an Indian) which had elicited some organised protest, although *not* from within Azariah's own diocese.

of authority and discipline in the newly organised churches. And finally Roland draws conclusions, emphasizing the contrast between the principles and spirit of St.Paul's methods, and those of contemporary missionary societies.

In the words of Roland's daughter, my Aunt Priscilla:

> *Here we have straightaway the prophetic, Hear the word of the Lord. He was not recommending a revolution, he said, but a return to first principles. This is how he began his book: In little more than ten years St. Paul established the Church in four Provinces of the Empire, Galatia, Macedonia, Achaia and Asia. Before AD 47 there were no churches in these provinces; in AD 57 St. Paul could speak as if his work there was done . . .* [12]

The facts are these, remarks Roland himself, later in the book: *St. Paul preached in a place for five or six months and then left behind him a Church, not indeed free from the need of guidance, but capable of growth and expansion.*

What a contrast with contemporary practice as described by Bishop Whitehead! *We found Churches and keep them in leading strings for a hundred years, and even then are not within measurable distance of giving them independence.*

> *We have done everything for them*, Roland points out, *We have taught them, baptized them, shepherded them. We have managed their funds, ordered their services, built their churches, provided their teachers. We have nursed them, fed them, doctored them . . . We have done everything for them except acknowledge any equality. We have done everything for them, but very little with them . . . We have treated them as 'dear children', but not as brethren.* [13]

---

[12] 'Roland Allen—a Prophet for this Age', *op. cit.*, pp. 9-11.

[13] *Missionary Methods*, pp. 113, ix, and 189f. [This book has appeared in various editions, and pagination is not consistent. Quotations in the present study refer to the original Robert Scott edition (London, 1912)].

Missionary Methods caused something of a stir when it was published, and has continued to exercise influence to this day. The book has been reprinted as recently as 1993, not as an historical curiosity, but as a valid textbook for contemporary missionaries and theologians. As an American Episcopalian once perceptively remarked:

> *no serious Churchman can read this extraordinary book without some sense of emotional shock. Although Allen is ostensibly discussing China, India and other far off places, one keeps having the uncomfortable feeling that he has a curiously intimate knowledge of one's own diocese or parish, one's own Sunday School class or prayer group, even of one's own devotional life.*[14]

Nevertheless, Roland felt frustrated and disappointed because, although the merits of his arguments were acknowledged, even people he greatly admired, such as his mentors at Pusey House, Bishop Charles Gore, and Father Waggett SSJE, seemed to be impervious to the need for change: *I could not understand how wise men could see what I saw and not change their whole manner of action.*[15]

The following year Roland supplemented *Missionary Methods* with a shorter treatise, entitled *Missionary Principles*, which still has such validity that in recent years it has been described as a *simple direct text book on how to be a missionary of Jesus Christ*— and not only in the overseas mission fields but *equally useful in Britain for the training of the 'house church' in the housing estate, or the 'cell' in the industrial or commercial corporation.* In this book, too, Roland was forthright in his condemnation of much misplaced enthusiasm:

> *world-wide missionary zeal is something very different from zeal for a society . . . Are there not clergy who, preferring a*

---

[14] Dr. H. Boone Porter in *The Living Church,* May 1963: cited by David Paton in *Reform of the Ministry, op. cit.*, p. 20f.

[15] *Church Missionary Review* (June 1927), p.148.

*society to missionary zeal, have quenched missionary zeal in
order to advance a society? Are there not laymen who have
put their pet society into the first place, so that unless their
missionary spirit could be expressed in and for that society it
vanished?* (p.50)

Roland was particularly concerned that such 'missionary
zeal' could easily make people forget that *the Church in its
entirety is a missionary body of which every member is a missionary.
There is thus no ground for the existence of a body of professional
missionaries in the New Testament.*[16]

This concern for missionary methods was to remain a
preoccupation for Roland for the rest of his life. In his Rhodes
Memorial Lecture of 1928, General Smuts was to propound that
missionaries in Africa had done much harm by their ignorance
of anthropology and psychology, so that *for the missionary, good
and bad and indifferent in native practice were met with the same ban,
so long as it was not in the Bible or the advanced practice of Christian
Europe.*[17]

Roland was sympathetic with such a plea for sensitivity to
local custom, although he did not fully agree with Smuts:

*What missionaries need is not so much a knowledge of these
sciences as a faith in the Gospel which they preach . . . a
deeper trust in the Holy Spirit to guide their converts, a
deeper conviction that the only secure advance is an internal
advance, rather than an external under direction from
without . . . The wisest of us is ignorant: the Holy Spirit
alone knows. The Gospel is the administration of the Spirit,
rather than the inculcation of Law.*[18]

Uncompromising criticism by Roland of their customary
work and methods would presumably have made him less and
less acceptable for deputation work on behalf of the missionary

---

[16]See Donald A. McGavran, *The Bridges of God* (World Dominion Press,
1955), p.12.

[17]See *The Times*, 18 November 1928, p. 19.

[18]Draft letter, 1928—unpublished.

societies, and less and less happy to undertake it. So it is hard to guess how he would have been able to support himself and his family, had his ideas not now attracted the attention of a wealthy Christian philanthropist, one S.J.W. Clark, whom Roland met in 1914.

Sidney Clark (1862-1930) was a layman, not a clergyman or a professional missionary, and a Congregationalist, not an Anglican. Starting in 1876 at the age of fourteen as an assistant in a pawnbroker's shop, where he was often obliged to sleep on the counter for want of any other home, he had worked his way up, until by 1907 he had become a rich man, the proprietor of a clothing business with eighty-nine branches.

Clark travelled extensively in the course of his business, and took a great interest in the work of overseas missions: a visit to Japan, Korea and China in 1905 made an especially deep impression on him, for he was both astonished by the lack of systematic planning and coordination, and shocked by what appeared to him to be gross inefficiency and wastage of resources. In his own words: *If I conducted my business in the way the missionary societies conduct theirs, I would be bankrupt.*

In 1907 Clark resigned from his business in order to give his whole time to the work of overseas missions. But, as Sir Kenneth Grubb points out, *No respectable society would have accepted him as a missionary. He was forty-five, and his education was scant: to the end of his days he found great difficulty in expressing himself coherently on paper.*[19] Furthermore, attempts by him to disseminate his ideas tended to be fruitless. The secretary of one missionary society remarked: 'When I get any of Clark's stuff it goes straight into the waste paper basket!'[20]

So Clark joined forces with two very different men.

---

[19]'The Story of the Survey Application Trust', *Reform of the Ministry, op. cit.*, p. 62.

[20]French, *op. cit.*, p.89.

CHAPTER VIII

The World Dominion Movement and World War I

'On the whole I think it was a fine wreck'
Royal Fleet Auxilliary 'Rohilla', October 1914

It was probably during his seminal first visit to China, in 1905, that Clark met Dr. Thomas Cochrane. This Presbyterian Scotsman had gone out with his wife to Chaoyang in eastern Mongolia in 1897, as a missionary doctor; and, after the Boxer Rising, had begun to build up the Peking Union Medical College.[1]

---

[1]Later taken over by the Rockefeller Health Foundation. For more details of Cochrane's life see Francesca French's biography (*op. cit.*).

Cochrane, like Clark, was shocked and concerned by what seemed to him to be the grossly unsystematic missionary effort in China. To bring this to wider attention he compiled an immensely detailed Survey of the Missionary Occupation of China, with an accompanying atlas.[2] In 1914 he returned to settle in Britain, where he lived until he died in 1953, at the age of eighty-seven.

During the First World War Sidney Clark worked first among refugees in Belgium, and then *as a special constable in London, volunteering for very disagreeable jobs.* But he seems to have found time to read and to reflect on his disquiet regarding missionary activities, and in consequence was profoundly influenced by two books, namely, by Ellis' *Madagascar Revisited,* a critical history of Christian missions on that island; and, especially, by Roland's *Missionary Methods—St. Paul's or Ours?* [3]

Both Clark and Cochrane had considerable faith in the value of surveys and quantitative research. Cochrane's survey and atlas were characteristic; and as Kenneth Grubb remarks, it was one of Clark's weaknesses that *he was apt to assume that, if only the facts of a situation could be uncovered, men would rush to remedy the obvious ills.*

Roland Allen was much more inclined to agree with Grubb's ensuing dry comment: *Unfortunately, men, even Christian men, do not so act.* Roland was sceptical about the value of surveys: *His attitude was, 'What are you doing where you are? Till you have set that on the right lines, what is the use of discovering and entering new fields to make the old mistakes?'* Furthermore, as he had long ago remarked of the missionaries in North China:

> *their work and its result should not be gauged by the mere bulk of it. Statistics—or what a man cannot do, or what a man wants to do—do not represent the work of a whole*

---

[2] The Survey, and *Atlas of China in Provinces showing Missionary Occupation,* were both published in 1913 by the Christian Literature Society for China.

[3] See Roland's portrait of his friend and benefactor: *Sidney James Wells Clark—a Vision of Foreign Missions,* pp. 107f.

man . . . the real value of the Mission lies not in what they do, or are compelled to leave undone . . . but that in God's time, and by His grace, that whole life must bear its fruit in the regeneration of China.[4]

Moreover, he was profoundly concerned about such matters as the ministry, the liturgy, and the sacraments, in which his future colleagues took much less interest than a relatively high church Anglican. Nevertheless, when he met the two Congregationalists in 1914, all three of them were united in their conviction that much of the Church's missionary effort was seriously misguided: what is more, all three shared *a deep concern for the place and pre-eminence of the Holy Spirit in all the work of the Church everywhere, and in the practical activities that this conviction involved.*[5] Their abilities complemented one another's: Clark's business acumen made him an excellent manager for the project; Cochrane's charm and sensitivity made him the team's diplomat; and Roland with his trained analytic mind and wide learning was their philosopher and theologian.

So in 1917 they joined together in setting up the World Dominion Movement, initially based in three small rooms on the top floor of No. 3, Tudor Street, in London's East End. These premises were rented by World Dominion from the National Laymen's Missionary Movement, for which Cochrane was then working.

The great foundation of their work, notes Cochrane's biographer, *was the basis which they liked to call the Three Supreme Loyalties:*

(i)   *To the Lord Jesus Christ and the centrality of His Cross.*
(ii)   *To the Bible as the final authority on Faith and Practice.*
(iii) *To the Lord's command to world-wide witness.*[6]

---

[4]*The Land of Sinim*, Vol.XII/3 (July 1904), p. 20.

[5]See Alexander McLeish, 'Biographical Memoir' in Paton, *Ministry of the Spirit, op. cit.,* pp. xii and xiii.

[6]French, *op. cit.,* p. 89f.

The following year the trio became the trustees of the precursor of the Survey Application Trust, with its publishing branch, the World Dominion Press. However, the original trust proved too restrictive in its terms. Moreover, Roland found the duties of a trustee excessively irksome; so when the Survey Application Trust itself was formed in 1918, Roland's place was taken by Cochrane's son—also a doctor, later to become well known as a leprologist.

The trust and the press were set up with the specific task (as laid down in the revised trust deed of 1927) of helping to apply, anywhere in the world, the principles asserted by Clark in his pamphlets and by Roland in his two best known books to that date, namely *Missionary Methods,* and *The Spontaneous Expansion of the Church.*[7] In the eyes of most people, these principles were no more than what were known as the 'indigenous principles' of evangelization and the expansion of the Church through self-support, self-propagation and self-government—principles which had been advocated as long ago as the middle of the nineteenth century by Henry Venn of the Church Missionary Society.[8] For Roland, however, these principles were simply an outward expression of something far more fundamental.

But before we go further, we must digress, to observe that during these same years the world had been going to war.

When the 1914-18 war broke out, Beatrice's elder brother, Alfred Tarleton, being a former naval officer, was recalled to the Admiralty. He had long been fully reconciled with his sister's marriage, and was able to secure for Granfer a post as naval chaplain in the Royal Fleet Auxiliary H.M.S. *Rohilla*, a British India liner converted for war duty as a hospital ship.

Roland hated the separation from his wife and children; but on the whole he enjoyed this assignment, apart from a long spell of boredom, waiting for sailing orders in the Firth of Forth. This

---

[7]Published in 1927, the year in which the Deed was drawn up.

[8]See e.g. Eugene Stock, *The History of the Church Missionary Society* (1899), Vol. 2, p. 83.

was only briefly alleviated by a visit from Beatrice, who left the two children in Oxford with their grandmother and the faithful Hannah.

One characteristic anecdote was told of Roland conducting a funeral on a remote Scottish island, after a crew member had died during a training exercise. When with considerable difficulty the coffin had been rowed ashore in rough seas, it was discovered that no-one had brought a prayer book: so Granfer proceeded to conduct the whole service—prayers, Bible readings and all—entirely from memory. The officer, who later recounted this to Grannie, told her that he looked up the service on his return to the ship: so far as he could make out, the chaplain's memory had been quite faultless. *And I don't think I've ever had a more attentive congregation*, remarked Granfer drily.

We may note in passing that Roland certainly did have an excellent verbal memory. His daughter, Priscilla, averred that he knew by heart almost all the Book of Common Prayer and much of the Bible. I can myself recall him reciting long passages from Homer, Virgil, and Robert Browning: he always quoted in the original, believing that the mere sound of poetry could convey meaning, even if the hearer did not know the language. One of my sisters remembers being told by him that poetry should always be read aloud, either sitting upright or standing. My own first conscious introduction to the true thrill of poetry was occasioned by some chance remark of mine, at the age of nine or ten, which prompted Granfer to declaim in his beautifully clear sonorous voice Shelley's sonnet, *Ozymandias*.

Roland's naval chaplaincy did not last long. At the end of October, 1914, on her way across to Dunkirk, to bring home wounded men from the Western Front, H.M.S. *Rohilla* went onto the rocks in heavy seas close to the north Yorkshire coast. Mercifully there were not yet any patients aboard, and the Whitby lifeboat succeeded in taking off all the nurses. Before many of the men on board could be rescued, however, the storm became fiercer, although a few strong swimmers succeeded in getting ashore. Every attempt to get a line out to the wreck by using a rocket proved unsuccessful: the ship broke in two, and all those left on the smaller half were soon swept away by a huge wave.

After another 24 hours a few more managed to swim ashore, but then the storm grew fiercer again. The captain, in fear that the ship would begin to disintegrate, asked for volunteers to try to swim ashore with a line. The first man to go was the quarter-master, a big man and a strong swimmer. He jumped well clear of the wreck: but those left on board simply watched his two legs spinning round and round in a whirlpool, and then the poor man disappeared; his body was later washed ashore.

Further volunteers were reluctant to come forward; so Granfer—'weak heart' and all—offered to make an attempt. Commending his soul to his Maker, he dived in and felt himself being sucked astern into the breakers; but he struck out for all he was worth until he got into smoother water and felt his feet touch sand. Then he fainted, but the fishermen's wives, watching from the shore, formed a human chain and dragged him in; several other swimmers then successfully followed his example, though none of them seems to have succeeded in bringing ashore a life-line. In all, only 146 of the 220 persons on board the *Rohilla* got ashore alive—plus the ship's cat *which appeared little the worse for its experience!* [9]

Brother-in-law Alfred managed to arrange for the Edinburgh express to make an unscheduled stop, so that Grannie could get to Roland's bedside in a fishing cottage, where she nursed his pneumonia until he was fit to be moved.

By no means all of this dramatic story emerges in Roland's vivid, but cheerfully self-deprecating, letter of reassurance to his wife's sister-in-law:

---

[9]*The Times*, 2 November 1914.

Nov.3.1914

My dear Ettie,

B has read your letter to me. Jolly good of you and A. I am still a bit 'off'. I got some water inside and had symptoms suggesting pneumonia. I shall be kept here for a day or two longer, then I hope to return home for a bit. The wreck was just an ordinary wreck, very much what I expected a wreck wd be like except (1) we all prepared for it before we left harbour (2) the ship broke much more rapidly than I expected (3) the chaplain's dive was quite beyond any of his earlier performances. It argues some great stupidity in the beholders that no mention of it was made in the papers. On the other hand the chaplain's swimming was not good. He allowed himself to be drifted into a nasty place out of which he escaped by no skill of his own (unless to keep one's head & to hang on is skill). Out of that he was cast into smooth water where a child cd scarcely have gone astray. So I came ashore full of water & rather sick. & just had sense to send B a telegram at once.

On the whole I think it was a fine wreck. The voyage from the moment that we got to sea was peculiarly rough. Most of us were more or less sick, & our cabins were dice boxes in wh all our effects were dice. I have seldom seen my bags so agile. That was Thurs evening. At 4 a.m. on Fr. we struck. It was the old story of Scylla & Charybdis. The Captain shied at the mine & struck on the rock. I took things quietly & dressed carefully. By that I scored: I did not suffer from cold as some did. Also I got a box of chocs which I doled out to the Sisters. We were on deck fr 4 a.m. till about 9.0. Then the Life boat reached us & we sent off two lots. By that time the ship was broken right across & the stern was carrying on an independent & hopeless existence with about 10 men clinging to the rail. Poor souls—they all went overboard with one great wave. Then we spent 24 hours watching people fire rockets, move about life boats, & such like, & watching, what was to me more novel, the way waves tear a ship to pieces. Of course we had nothing to eat or drink. But I did not hear anyone complain of hunger or thirst. About 8 a.m. next morning we were still there, (i.e. the bridge had held out against the rising tide again) & another Life boat made an attempt to get at us. But oars were no use. They were simply carried to & fro. Then men began in numbers to try to swim ashore—a few had gone the night before. The Captain seemed to desire that as many as could shd go that way. I went about 9.0. As I look back I do not think there was any terrible danger. If a man kept his head, if he kept off the rocks, if he struck the stream he was practically safe. I admit that when I drifted astern & got into those breakers & was beaten & tossed I gave up all hope. I felt certain that the next wave would see me finished. I have never been quite so dead as I was then. But my mind was perfectly clear & calm & I could review the situation both as it affected B & the children & myself with a curious clearness & a positively delightful confidence. I cd almost say that I enjoyed it.

About 25 bodies have been recovered, there must be more somewhere. Not all who swam reached the shore. All who stayed on the ship (Except the poor folk in the stern) got off. The Bridge held up another 24 hrs & then a motor lifeboat took them all off.

Now I am jolly well tired. Let this suffice. I hope Alfred will hold out. I do not know when I shall get another ship. I wish you wd send this to my brother, the Archd at 34 Carew Rd, Eastbourne. I cannot write it again just now.

Yrs affly

Roland Allen

Regretfully invalided out of the Navy after this episode, Roland recuperated at home in Harpenden in Hertfordshire, acting for many months as the temporary curate-in-charge of St. John's Church there. For a while, in 1916, he crossed to France to serve with the YMCA in Rouen, although all that anyone in the family can recall of this sojourn is his irritation at being required to wear the ribbon of the China Medal, which had been awarded to him for his service as chaplain in the British Legation at Peking during the siege. The medal itself had been lost when *Rohilla* went down, but the War Office sent him another one.

From the autumn of 1917 until the end of the war, Roland took on the job of senior classical master at the King's School, Worcester. He and his family lived at 5 Battenhall Road, not very far from the school. Evidently he reverted to his enthusiasm for visual aids, for the school magazine records him giving a lantern lecture on 'The Boxer Rising'. He left in December 1918 *to take up secretarial work in connection with Christian Missions, where his personal experiences and advice will prove a valuable asset to those in authority.*[10]

Worcester Cathedral adjoins the school, and he was alleged to have been temporarily appointed an honorary minor canon; but there are no records of this in the chapter archives. Certainly he often took boys into the cathedral for services, presumably as assistant to the school chaplain.

On the terrible day when news came through from the Western Front that the Worcestershire Regiment had been almost wiped out, many people made their way spontaneously into the cathedral. Granfer was among them and apparently led an impromptu service, including an address so moving and uplifting that—even in those ghastly circumstances—the assembled congregation joined with a will in the hymn *Now thank we all our God.* Shopkeepers three blocks away could hear the singing.

---

[10]See *The Vigornian,* November 1917 and March 1919: I am grateful to Mr M.R. Craze, Hon. Secretary of the Old Vigornian Club, for these data.

It seems that Roland's manner of preaching was arresting and inspiring. At the time of his resignation from Chalfont St. Peter, someone remarked that:

As a preacher Mr. Allen is unconventional, frank and daring. It is impossible to hear him even once without realising that his are no second-hand conclusions. His experiences at Peking have made him impatient of nearly all formal and nominal Christianity.[11]

Moreover, people used to say that when he spoke it often seemed to them that he was addressing concerns, which they thought were their private worries. And a Kenya settler was to write to him many years later:

You say that you, yourself, cannot comprehend God, and yet to me you are the only person I have met who is so near comprehending what God is.

Roland kept meticulous notes,[12] with quotations in Greek or in Hebrew or even in Chinese; and he often wrote out his sermons in full, although he practically never read from the prepared script. Indeed, on more than one occasion he was moved to abandon it altogether, disconcerting his congregation with some such comment as: *This doesn't seem to be getting us anywhere, does it? Let's take another text, and start again!*—whereupon he would often produce a particularly memorable and heartfelt homily.

A few of Roland's sermons were reprinted, but these were mostly uncharacteristic 'set pieces', such as the Oxford University Ramsden Sermon for 1919, in which he admonished such scholars as Professor Sweete, Hutchings, and Bishops Welldon, Moberly, Webb and Moule for failure to trust in the revelation of the Holy Spirit. One readily available example of Roland's

---

[11]'A Special Contributor' writing in *The Church Family Newspaper*, 20/12/1907.

[12]A great many of these, usually with indication of their place and date, are preserved among the Roland Allen papers in Oxford's Rhodes House.

pulpit elegance is his admonitory address to the Diocesan Synod of Pretoria, which, exceptionally, he read from a pre-pared text in consequence of his anxiety to use no word that he had not *meditated on and prayed over*.[13] Even if few actual sermons survive in full, however, his written style often reveals the preacher, being alight with rhythm, rhetorical questions, emphatic repetitions, and the like.

He seems to have preached in several cathedrals, for I recall him remarking on one occasion that *Of all the cathedrals I've had to preach in, Ripon was the worst for acoustics.* He was always a stickler for clarity of diction: I can remember being reproved by him for 'mumbling'; and my sisters recollect his teaching them to whisper audibly across an open-air summerhouse. Both his own children had extremely clear speaking voices. At Westminster School, in 1923, Iohn won the prize for 'Orations', beating John Gielgud into second place! As for Priscilla, her voice could often be embarrassing, as her faultless enunciation on the telephone carried clearly right across the room: *Do you mean your visitor is that woman who wears those extraordinarily ugly hats?*

In spite of all these wartime duties and distractions, some of Roland's most productive thinking and writing took place in the course of these years. For example, he set out to study modern educational theories, in order to supplement *Missionary Methods* from another point of view, and that the most remote from the earlier one. He wrote this book as a deliberate attempt to counter one of the criticisms of *Missionary Methods*—namely, *that the gulf between the people to whom we go is deeper and wider than that between St.Paul and those to whom he preached*; in *Educational Principles & Missionary Methods* Roland argued that *the greater the gulf, the greater was the value of the apostolic method.*[14]

---

[13]Printed in *The East & the West:* April 1927, pp. 123-133: see Chapter XI below.

[14]Author's preface to the 2nd (1927) edition of *Missionary Methods: St.Paul's or Ours?*

Like the former book, these ideas were first published in Robert Scott's series *The Library of Historic Theology*. Bishop Charles Gore was persuaded to contribute a far from enthusiastic introduction, commenting privately—though in a letter signed *Yours affectionately—I wonder if this very poor preface, which expresses my feeling, will raise anything in your mind except disgust.*[15]

It is curious, noted Roland in this new book, *how often the application of modern educational principles leads us to the same conclusion which the study of St. Paul's methods suggested. His practice seems often nearer than our own to the most modern educational theory.* Roland sought to demonstrate how the ideas of such educationalists as Pestalozzi, Froebel and Montessori sought to escape from rote-learning, and first and foremost to assist the child to observe facts, truly and fully:

> *Knowledge of facts and theories,* acknowledged Roland, *is very different from knowledge of a person: the teaching of facts is very different from the revelation of a person. If then knowledge of facts must be based upon the sure foundation of sense perception, knowledge of a person must be based upon a firm foundation of spiritual perception. To be continually preaching about a person the reality of whose existence has never been perceived is even more hopeless than to teach the science of mathematics to pupils who have never perceived the meaning of number . . .*

> *Why do we live in perpetual terror lest the religious teaching which we have given to our children, and to our converts in the mission field, should be overthrown by some specious argument . . .? Surely it is because we are fearful lest our religious instruction may have been built on no solid foundation; but has been merely intellectual education which is liable to be overthrown by a clever intellectual attack . . .*

> *At present,* concluded Roland, *the Catechisms, the*

---

[15]Undated letter from 7 Margaret Street, London W.

Lord's Prayer, the Ten Commandments and the Creed. . . are taught by the same methods, as the three R's in the unreformed schools before Pestalozzi was born.

This approach to Christian teaching and evangelism, both at home and in the overseas mission fields, arose, Roland suggested, from a fundamental lack of faith:

the difficulty is for us to believe in the indwelling Spirit . . . To trust the Spirit seems to us a desperate act . . . We are indeed afraid of liberty. We are afraid of it because we do not know what our converts would do if they were at liberty . . . we have no real confidence that they would continue to employ the forms which we have imposed upon them.[16]

These words demonstrate what one of Granfer's most perceptive critics has described as *the high and lofty significance which Allen ascribed to the Holy Spirit.* Many superficial discussions of his work have suggested that Roland's concern was principally with the 'indigenous method' and that his importance was simply that he saw the merits of this earlier than other people.

It is true, of course, that Roland's thinking about the 'indigenous method' was very influential. Half a century later, for example, Bishop Stephen Neill was to write:

. . . all over the world there are in existence today independent and self-governing Younger Churches . . . In part this change is linked to the political changes . . . But the change is also due to the vision of a certain number of prophets, among them Roland Allen . . .[17]

Nevertheless, to suggest that this was Roland's primary message, protests Harry R. Boer, is *not just wrong, but completely wrong. Completely wrong because its close approximation to the truth obscures . . . the one thing that he wanted most desperately to say, and to the saying of which he devoted so much of his energy over so long a period of time.*

---

[16]*Educational Principles & Missionary Methods, op, cit.,* pp. vii, 61, 72f., 119.
[17]Neill, *op. cit.,* p. 418.

Educational Principles & Missionary Methods was not published until the war was over. However, the one small book—little more than a pamphlet—which he did publish during the war, expressed even more forcefully that 'high and lofty significance'. This little study of The Acts of the Apostles, entitled *Pentecost and the World*, was in Roland's own opinion the best single piece of work he ever wrote: on his death, for this reason, Grannie gave bound copies to each of us, his three grandchildren. Certainly it provides a true epitome of his fundamental beliefs and ideas. In the words of the critic just mentioned:

Allen's observations in this booklet leave little doubt that he had a truer appreciation of what Luke really meant to say in his account of the outpouring of the Spirit than many learned exegetes who have spent their skill in analyzing it.[18]

The writer has made use of this little book for a Bible study group in the 1990s; and its members were unanimous in their testimony that *Pentecost and the World* can speak to us today as cogently as when it was written, over three-quarters of a century ago.

---

[18]Harry R. Boer, 'Roland Allen, the Holy Spirit, and Missions', *World Dominion*, XXXIII/5 (September-October 1955), pp. 298-300.

CHAPTER IX

Peace and Beaconsfield

'the splendour of the Tarleton family home'
'Breakspears', Hertfordshire, c. 1930

Pentecost & the World and an article, using the sub-title of this book as its title and seeking to consolidate its arguments,[1] both examine *The Revelation of the Holy Spirit in the Acts of the Apostles*. In this study Roland pays little attention to puzzling questions that have tended to exercise the minds of other scholars. Of the 'speaking with other tongues', for example, he comments:

Much learned ingenuity has been spent in attempts to explain what exactly happened ... To me, I confess, these discussions seem to be curiously interesting [sic] and

---

[1] *International Review of Missions* (April 1918).

unprofitable, and their conclusions equally dubious and
barren. They tend rather to divert the mind, and to lead it
away from the point of real significance and importance . . .

That 'point of real significance' Roland describes
thus: *The fact, clear and unmistakable, is that the Apostles,*
when the Holy Spirit descended upon them, began at once to
address themselves to men out of every nation and language,
and that the Spirit enabled them so to speak that men
understood. Thus, at His first coming, the Holy Spirit
revealed His nature and His work as world-wide, all-
embracing. He revealed His work as enabling those to whom
He came to preach Christ to men of every nation.

Throughout his work, and quintessentially in this little
book, suggests Harry Boer, Roland's *deepest and abiding signifi-*
cance lies in the perspectives that he opened by taking seriously the
scriptural teaching that Pentecost is the source of all true missionary
power and advance.[2]
Such perspectives included, for example, a foreshadowing
of the Ecumenical Movement in his protestation about the
absurdity of disunity among Christians:

If the Holy Ghost is given, those to whom He is given are
certainly accepted in Christ by God . . . Men may separate
them, systems may part them from the enjoyment and
strength of their unity; but, if they share the one Spirit, they
are one.

Pentecost & the World was not really 'rediscovered' until it
was given a prominent place in *The Ministry of the Spirit,* David
Paton's anthology of selections from Roland's shorter writings,
which was published in 1960. But this *high and lofty significance*
which Allen ascribed to the Holy Spirit is expressed again and again
in all his writings, and not least in the only book other than

---

[2]Harry R. Boer, 'Roland Allen, the Holy Spirit, and Missions', *World*
Dominion, XXXIII/5 (September-October 1955), p. 303. See also *Pentecost & the*
World, pp. 42f, 85.

Missionary Methods that during his lifetime was at all widely read. This was rather ponderously entitled *The Spontaneous Expansion of the Church, and the Causes which Hinder It*. It was published by the World Dominion Press in 1927.

'Sponx', as Roland's family irreverently called it, was described by Bishop Azariah in his introduction as *a clarion call to all missionary Bishops, Missionaries, and Missionary Societies once more carefully to examine the methods followed in the mission field for evangelization, and for the building up of the Church*. In it Roland pursued still further his constant theme that Christ came to bring, not Law, but the Holy Spirit:

> *Every attempt to treat any of His sayings as legal enactments has always resulted in confusion, and error, and, what is far worse, in the letting loose of a flood of ill-will, hatred, pride, and self-righteous pharisaism which is the direct contradiction of His Spirit . . . The revelation of a higher code of morals is no Gospel.*

Twentieth century tendencies to transform Christianity into no more than 'a code of morals'—a mere system of doctrine and practice—thought Roland, had (as one consequence) a gross over-emphasis on non-spiritual requirements:

> *Instead of establishing the Church and then assisting in its education, we insist that the education and civilization must come before the establishment of the Church . . . an elaborate internal machinery for the propagation of ideas seems to most of those to whom we go almost absurd. You do not want buildings and machinery to propagate ideas or a faith; you want ideas and a faith.*

That faith should lead us, Roland passionately believed, into handing over to people what F.D. Maurice called the 'Signs of the Kingdom'—the Creed, the Bible, the Ministry, and the Sacraments—and then leaving the Church's further growth to the Holy Spirit, without seeking constantly to train and to control:

*The wind bloweth where it listeth, said Christ, and spontane-
ous activity is a movement of the Spirit in the individual and
in the Church, and we cannot control the Spirit.*[3]

Anxieties about the possibility of irregularities and doctri-
nal error were brushed aside by him in a letter to The Church
Times (30 May 1924):

*Am I not right in saying that in the early centuries of the
Christian era the dangers to the Faith, the dangers to unity,
arose not from the illiterate bishops, but from the highly
educated? And would not the free ordination of natives and
the establishment of real churches, obviously and unques-
tionably purely native, as a matter of fact tend to cut the
ground from under the feet of the malcontents, whose
argument is that we white men keep all authority in our own
hands?*

In 'Sponx', and in many of his articles and pamphlets published by the Survey Application Trust, Roland keeps stressing
that the primary task of every missionary should be the propagation of the Gospel. He was by no means opposed to the involvement of Christians in social concerns, such as the provision of
schools and hospitals: indeed this was, in his view, an important
part of the mission of the laity. But for the missionary as
evangelist, he believed, those tasks must be secondary.

As he thought about these matters, Roland began to observe
that they led to further consequences. His daughter once remarked that *There are three themes in the life of Roland Allen which
overlap like the tunes in a fugue.*[4] He had been a missionary, and
had found that lack of faith in the Spirit was damaging overseas
missionary enterprise. He had been a parish priest, and had
found that lack of faith in the Spirit was damaging the Church
of England. He was still an ordained priest—and now he was

---

[3]*The Spontaneous Expansion of the Church* (World Dominion Press, 1962), pp.
91f., 155, and 16.

[4]'Roland Allen—A Prophet for this Age', *op. cit.*, p. 9.

beginning to question whether lack of faith in the Spirit was not damaging the Church's sacramental ministry itself. These thoughts led him on to the third theme in the fugue.

Soon after the First World War, S.J.W. Clark provided for Granfer and his family a house, called 'Amenbury', in Beaconsfield, a small market town west of London. He also provided an annual honorarium of £ 200, in order that Roland would be able to 'devote himself entirely to the study of foreign missions'.

The Allens, relatively elderly and set in their ways when they married, did not find it easy to 'socialize' outside their own family, though they kept up in particular with a few of the friends of Grannie's youth, such as the well-known authoress of Bible stories for children—C.P.S. Warren (Mrs. Watkin Williams)—whose son and daughter were among the two children's closest friends.

Besides these the principal intimates of Priscilla and Iohn were their young first cousins, the children of Grannie's sister. Both families used to cycle to and fro over the twenty miles between Beaconsfield and Weybridge, where Edith and her family had their home: *Roland was a very kind and lively and amusing uncle to have,* recalls Edith's daughter. Sometimes, too, Iohn and Priscilla would go to visit their Uncle Willoughby, or stay in his rectory at Chorley in Lancashire, especially when Roland was looking after the parish during his frail brother's increasingly frequent illnesses.

Occasionally they would visit Grannie's brother, their Uncle Alfred, in the splendour of the Tarleton family home at Breakspears between St. Alban's and Hemel Hempstead. This was nearer than Weybridge: but they had very little in common with the more conventional Tarleton girls, Freda, Vera and Helen, and, although fond of their Aunt Ettie, were rather in awe of her. Their favourite personality in that household seems to have been Gilbey, the butler, who would apparently have been a perfect prototype for Jeeves himself.

Apart from such visits the little family tended to live a

somewhat reclusive existence on a rather elevated intellectual plane. Almost all their close friends were theologians, notably Herbert Hamilton Kelly of the Society of the Sacred Mission at Kelham, Cosmo Gordon Lang (then Archbishop of York), and Canon Temple Gairdner of Cairo and his family. Others were scholars such as Oxford's Professor Gilbert Murray of St.John's and his wife, Lady Mary, one of Beatrice's girlhood friends, David Seth-Smith, the Director of the London Zoo, at whose home Iohn lived whilst in the sixth form at Westminster School, and Sir Charles Holmes, the Curator of London's National Gallery, whose son Martin (also at Westminster) was one of Iohn's closest friends.

My father also remembered another distinguished friend, one of their near neighbours in Beaconsfield, coming over to Amenbury one day, proudly exhibiting a letter from Argentina that had been correctly delivered to him by the Post Office, although all that was written on the envelope was —

G.K.
U.K.

This person was, of course, the renowned essayist, novelist and critic, G.K. Chesterton. Granfer enjoyed Chesterton's Father Brown stories: but he and his neighbour found their theological views were so divergent that it was better to refrain from discussions that would have been only acrimonious.

In earlier days, reminisces one of his nephews, Roland *like many Victorian and Edwardian Englishmen seemed to me to have a hearty and robust tendency towards puns, jokes, practical jokes, backslapping and teasing.* In his old age almost all such boisterousness vanished, although certainly he and his children rejoiced in puns and verbal witticisms. I can vividly remember their delight in limericks: not, of course, the notoriously lewd and scatalogical kind, but those that were dependent on word-play, such as the man of Japan, the lady of Spain, or the curate of Salisbury, and Dean Inge's curate of Kidderminster.[5]

Priscilla attended local day schools for girls—latterly Beaconsfield's Oakdene School. She had inherited something of her father's rebelliousness. One of her cousins recalls how she went through a phase of defiant agnosticism. Her mother, the conventional Beatrice, used to be very shocked when Priscilla would ostentatiously leave the room before grace at family meals, and return only after it had been said. Roland, on the contrary, was not at all upset by someone standing on principle, however much he disagreed with that principle.

Nevertheless, Priscilla to the end of her days felt that she had been let down by her parents. Beatrice tended to combine the austerity of rigid Victorian discipline with the rather smotheringly protective love that can be characteristic of those

---

[5]These triviata may bear repeating, for those to whom they are unfamiliar:

There was a young man of Japan,
who wrote verses that no-one could scan;
When they said this was so,
He replied: 'Yes, I know,
but I always like to get as many words into the last line as I possibly can.'

There once was a curate of Salisbury,
whose conduct was quite halisbury-scalisbury:
He ran about Hampshire
without any pampshire,
Till his Vicar compelled him to walisbury.
(NOTE: the abbreviations for 'Salisbury' and 'Hampshire' are respectively 'Sarum' and 'Hants')

There was a poor lady of Spain,
who was horribly sick in a train:
not once, but again,
and again, and again,
and again, and again, and again.

There once was a curate of Kidderminster,
who very regretfully chid a spinster:
For one day, on the ice,
she used words not quite nice
when he quite inadvertently slid aginst'er.

111

who become mothers late in life. Roland was devoted to all his family: his nickname for Priscilla—'Trusty'—showed his warm confidence in her. But his all-consuming dedication to his work, she felt, often led him unthinkingly to subordinate his family's happiness to his mission. His attitude to herself, she suggested, was that provided her family's love were assured she should feel the need of nothing more.

In consequence—she was wont to complain in later life— she and Iohn found themselves isolated from outside friend-ships, so that she in particular became painfully shy and self-consciously gauche, and had immense difficulty in relating to people outside her family circle. *How did you expect to get a determined & courageous woman out of the child I was, unless you took urgent steps to help me to become independent & self-reliant?* she protests in a letter to her father as late as 1942: *Even Oxford can't work miracles!*

These problems remained with her throughout her univer-sity career and continued until she was in her mid-thirties, when during the Second World War she found herself thrust into wider contacts, firstly in the Land Army, and then in the WAAF, where she at last attained so much self-confidence that she became a commissioned officer.

Iohn also suffered from this isolation, but less acutely than his sister. He submitted more readily than Priscilla to his domi-nating parents. Moreover, at twelve years of age he was sent off to boarding school, first near Brighton, and then to Marlborough College, where scholarships were available for the children of clergy. He was intensely unhappy at Marlborough, as is appar-ent from his correspondence in later years with his only true friend in the school, Max Warren, later to become the long-serving General Secretary of the Church Missionary Society. But the principal reason for his misery seems to have been that his parents' upbringing had made him rather priggish, with a horror of his boarding house's pervasive culture of pederasty that was almost pathological.

112

At length Roland and Beatrice discovered how wretched their son was at Marlborough. So, after an unsatisfactory correspondence with the headmaster, and with much help from Beatrice's brother, Alfred, they succeeded in taking him away, and sending him instead to live with the Seth-Smith family at the London Zoo in Regent's Park, from which he was able to attend the sixth and seventh forms at Westminster School as a day-boarder. There he was very much happier. He entered fully into the life of the school, and even took up rowing, becoming quite a respectable oarsman both there and later at St. John's, where he won his oar in the Torpid races.

Even in the 1920s two hundred pounds a year was not much of an income for a family of four, nor were their handful of shares in Chinese railways a very fruitful investment. Forty years' later Priscilla would write: *I, of course, have never been able to shake off the miserly habits I acquired in youth.*

Grannie's small inheritance from her aristocratic forebears helped to keep the four of them going in times of real poverty. However, her only valuables of any significance were lost *when the family tried to be careful; we weren't really meant to have possessions*, as my father once remarked, quoting Granfer. For example, Beatrice's 18th century Russian jewellery, inherited through her mother from the 4th Baron Dimsdale, was stolen from Amenbury in the mid-1920s, during the one and only night that it had been brought there from the bank to be valued for insurance. Those thieves were never apprehended, although a less competent burglar of Amenbury was caught and imprisoned: Roland used to visit 'my burglar' regularly in gaol, and became quite fond of him.

A very large quantity of postage stamps, from all over the world, had been amassed by Beatrice's father, Sir Walter, when he was serving in the Admiralty in the 1870s, at a time when very few people were yet interested in such things. This rich collection, still unsorted, was put into a bank by Granfer in 1936, for safe keeping: the bank was in Jersey, in the Channel Islands, so

113

presumably the Germans took them, for no record of them could be found there when the Second World War came to an end.

It follows that the Allens must have been glad when Clark's small honorarium began to be supplemented by fees for teaching. The first such fees were paid by a classmate of Priscilla's at Beaconsfield's Oakdene School. This young lady, a Miss Winifred Brooke, had made up her mind to try to get into Oxford University. She was a gifted linguist, speaking Spanish, French and English, having spent her childhood in Mexico and France: but at that time Oxford still insisted that all entrants pass an examination in Latin. One of her neighbours suggested that she consult this retired clergyman, so—braving the Allens' notoriously aggressive bantam cockerel—'Winkie' went round to inquire, and Roland came to the door himself: *Latin lessons? Why, yes, I suppose so. Come in now and we'll try . . .*

To start with, Roland's method of teaching was for the two of them to read through Latin texts together, without any kind of explanation or translation. Winkie recalled that he used to clutch his head in both hands and slide down his chair, groaning with disbelief at his pupil's appalling intellectual ignorance. She found this, and his blazing blue eyes, quite terrifying. Her younger sister was so scared of him that she used to hurt herself deliberately by falling off her bicycle, so as to avoid being sent to Amenbury.

Even if they were unorthodox and intimidatory, however, Granfer's teaching methods proved successful. So my mother went up to St. Hugh's College a few months' later, in the same term that Roland's and Beatrice's son Iohn began his own studies at his father's Oxford college, St. John's. Although mutually attracted, the two young people made an agreement not to meet while at Oxford, so that neither would be distracted from the full enjoyment of university life.

Like Winkie, other young people found Roland alarming, but helpful. *He got really angry with me about religion,* relates one of his nephews, *and thumped the desk, and shouted: but I knew he was my friend and really wanted to help my teenage doubts and*

114

embarrassments. For example, when I told him I was ashamed because I was getting sexy feelings, which I supposed were very sinful (I was thinking of Matthew 5:28), he said: No, they're not wrong, because they are natural. Don't worry unless you do something wrong.

Her schoolfriend's success emboldened Iohn's sister, Priscilla, to persuade Roland and Beatrice to allow her, too, to try for Oxford. So the following year she followed Winkie to St. Hugh's, like her brother to read 'Mods & Greats'—the classics and philosophy in the School of *Literae Humaniores*. She would have much preferred to study medicine, but her parents dissuaded her, since she had long been unable to bear the sight of blood. (In later years, however, she was apt to complain that their real reason had been Grannie's view that medicine was not a truly ladylike profession).

Meanwhile, Roland continued to work with—or at least alongside—his colleagues in the Survey Application Trust. He steadfastly refused to try to perform the duties of a trustee, so the team was joined by the Revd. Alexander McLeish, a Church of Scotland missionary, who had been involved in comparable survey work in his editing of the pioneering *Directory of Churches and Missions in India* for the National Christian Council of India. McLeish became Survey Editor for the Trust in 1926, shortly before its founder, S.J.W. Clark, became terminally ill.[6]

Roland's own health at this time seems to have been excellent. In 1925, for example, in the summer before Priscilla went up to Oxford University, he and his daughter cycled from Beaconsfield to Cheltenham, and on to visit his brother Reginald at Blakeney in Gloucestershire. Thence they proceeded to Crickhowell, where they succeeded in finding the 83-year-old landlady of the inn in which Beatrice and Roland had spent their honeymoon. And from there they set off on their well-laden bicycles right across the rugged country of central Wales to Cardigan Bay, and back home again through Shropshire, sometimes covering more than

---

[6]Alexander McLeish later returned to live in India, but remained one of the Trustees until his death in 1962, at the age of eighty-four.

forty miles a day. Only once does Roland seem to have felt physically frail, when he wrote to Beatrice on a postcard from Aberdovey:

> *They told us we could get a ferry across the estuary: they did not tell us that we should have to walk a couple of miles over loose sand, well over our shoes & the cycles sinking deep—a most horrid grind. My breath utterly gave out & I struggled along groaning and gasping . . . I never want to do that again.*

CHAPTER X

Non-Professional Missionaries

Amenbury, in Beaconsfield

One of the first activities of the Survey Trust was to issue a new quarterly journal, entitled *World Dominion*,[1] to which Roland was a principal contributor throughout the 1920s. Several of these contributions were reprinted as pamphlets in the movement's Indigenous Church Series, and others in its General Series and Medical Series. But it is noteworthy that his only contribution to the Survey Series (which for Clark and Cochrane was really the principal *raison d'être* of their whole movement)

---

[1] This journal was published regularly until 1958, when it was merged with *The Christian Newsletter*, under the title *Frontier*.

was to share with Cochrane in the writing of the introductory study—Missionary Survey as an Aid to Intelligent Cooperation in Foreign Missions.

Thereafter Roland made no written contribution to the surveys, and Sir Kenneth Grubb tells us that his lack of interest in these, and his insistence that the resources of the Trust should be devoted primarily to the propagation of the 'indigenous principles', became a cause of increasing conflict with Cochrane, who after Clark's death discontinued the £200 honorarium, which it had been arranged that the Trust should continue to pay Roland. Roland and Beatrice were much too proud to protest.

Roland (correctly) pointed out that the Trust Deed makes no mention of these surveys; [2] but Cochrane argued with equal force that they had been a principal motivation for his own participation, and for Clark to have invested so much of his personal fortune in the enterprise. Roland unhesitatingly made use of Survey money to travel abroad, to Canada, Southern Rhodesia, South Africa, and India: but, even though he was repeatedly asked to do so, his concern was not to carry out surveys: *You might as well have asked Stephen to survey the spread of Judaism in the Roman Empire as ask me to write a survey.*[3]

---

[2]The relevant parts of the main operating clause of the Deed charge the Trustees as follows:

'to promoting or assisting to promote the establishment overseas (particularly in rural areas) of Christian communities which when established will provide and maintain their own properties and religious activities from their own resources and which will in turn promote similar Christian communities and so foster the continuous growth of the Christian Church throughout the world. And in executing this trust the Trustees shall look for guidance to the principles enunciated by the founder of this Charity Sidney James Wells Clark in his series of pamphlets on the indigenous church and the books entitled Missionary Methods St Paul's or Ours? *and* The Spontaneous Expansion of the Church *by Roland Allen, MA and other literature already published by the Trustees in support of these principles.'* [Sir Kenneth Grubb, *op. cit.*, p. 68.]

[3]Letter to Alexander McLeish, 28 January 1932; McLeish himself cites an almost identical remark: see *The Ministry of the Spirit*, p. xv.

Had he been so minded, there is no question that he could have produced very detailed surveys, as can be seen from the thoroughness of his research into the meagre impact of 'the Archbishop's Western Canada Fund', during *several months making diligent enquiry* in 1924:

> *I had to interview men who had been on the spot throughout the whole period; I had to sift conflicting and sometimes contradictory statements; I had to study masses of local magazines, and to trace carefully the history of individual parishes, and the movements of individual members of the Mission. I travelled to the Pacific and back by different routes . . . I gave myself wholly to this one thing.*

In southern Africa in 1926, and back in India again in 1927/28, Roland demonstrated equal diligence. Soon after he and Beatrice went off to settle in Kenya, the Times of East Africa published his 'Survey of the Constitution of the Anglican Church in Kenya.' But, notwithstanding Cochrane's requests, all these studies were in pursuit of what Roland thought to be important, not in preparation of any of the purely factual surveys favoured by the Survey Application Trust. *My visit to Assam,* he admitted to Cochrane, *was not quite the work which you wanted done for the office. The office enabled me to do it, and I was certain that it was work which was within the terms; but I doubt if you were.*[4]

What Roland thought important was essentially a problem for Anglican and other episcopal churches in the catholic tradition, namely: *a great stream of spiritual power running to waste, while the bishops, instead of using it, are appealing feebly for money.*[5] During his tours in Rhodesia and South Africa from May to November 1926, and in southern India and Assam at the end of 1927 and early in 1928, his concerns and his theme remained constant—and they were not to do with surveys.

---

[4]Letter of 19 April 1928.

[5]*The Case for Voluntary Clergy, op. cit.,* p. 189; and letter in *Church Times* (5.12.1924)

One of the ways in which Roland differed from Cochrane was in diplomacy. Roland was frank about this:

I would not on any account (even if I could, and I know that I could not) draw you from your predestined course of 'festina lente' . . . 'never antagonize'; but for myself I am for 'the root of the matter' or 'cut to the bone', or let us get as near to the fundamental truth as our under-standing . . . will permit. The result is that you inevitably are a little afraid of what I may write—and justly . . .

One of Roland's most penetrating attacks on the church's waste of spiritual power was almost lost to us in consequence of his disagreements with the more diplomatically inclined Cochrane. Early in 1929 the World Dominion Press printed a new pamphlet by Roland entitled 'Missionaries Professional and Non-Professional'; it was to appear in their Indigenous Church Series. However, a handwritten note in one of those printed copies, which was preserved by him, observes that:

This pamphlet, after being printed, was withdrawn (by D/r/ C/o/c/h/r/a/n/e/ W.D.Press) because some Society Secretary saw it & objected to it as contrary to their policy. The edition was then given to me by Dr. Cochrane with all W.D. references extracted.

R.A. July 25, 1929

Fortunately for posterity, Roland felt so strongly about its contents that he issued it himself, re-entitled simply 'Non-Professional Missionaries', under his home address Amenbury, Beaconsfield, Bucks; and it has since been reprinted in *The Ministry of the Spirit*.

It is easy to see why the missionary society secretary was disturbed by the pamphlet, although Roland bases his arguments partly on concerns expressed by an eminent missionary, Canon Temple-Gairdner of Cairo, and protests in his preface: *I know devoted missionaries. I have neither the will nor the desire to hurt them; for I profoundly respect them. They will not be hurt . . . nothing*

120

that anyone may say can diminish their glory. But whilst he admired so many missionaries, he admired much less a great part of their work. As Bishop Lesslie Newbigin noted, Roland considered that missionaries should confine themselves strictly to transmitting 'the Signs of the Kingdom'—the Bible, the Creed, the Sacraments of Baptism and Holy Communion, and the Ministry:

> *He waged war against everything that missions had tried to bring apart from these—the whole apparatus of a professional ministry, institutions, church buildings, church organizations, diocesan offices and all the rest of it—everything from harmoniums to archdeacons.*[6]

In 'Non-Pro Mish', as the family called it, Roland addresses more emphatically than ever before the issue that had first begun to worry him some thirty years earlier: the impact of *the conduct of foreign merchants and engineers travelling in the interior*; and the fact that, according to Paul's teaching, *every* Christian ought to be a missionary, and *ought to be a missionary in his ordinary daily work, all the time, not merely outside it, and part of the time . . . When we draw our modern distinction between 'missionary work' and 'secular work', we divide life precisely as the Apostle taught us not to divide it.*

In consequence of this teaching of St. Paul, in Roland's view: *It is necessary that men with strong missionary convictions should go out deliberately into distant lands as officials and farmers and traders.* It was lamentable that *the great Societies think that they cannot afford to support any such movement* because of their anxiety to divert Christians from 'secular work' to 'missionary work'—*as if 'missionary work' were a special occupation, as specialized as banking or mining or farming.*

Alongside this concern with 'professional missionaries' being singled out as a class apart, Roland was giving expression more and more to another concern: the presumption—as serious, in his opinion, at home in England as abroad in the mission

---

[6]In an article on 'Conversion' in *Religion & Society*, XIII/4 (Bangalore): cited by Paton, *Reform of the Ministry, op, cit.*, p. 41.

field—that the administration of the sacraments of the Church could and should be restricted to a narrowly defined class, set apart as 'professional clergy'. Apart from occasionally helping to look after his brother's parishes when Willoughby was ill, Roland in fact spent most of the rest of his active career absorbed in this question of 'voluntary clergy'— so single-mindedly that, as he ruefully noted, episcopal eyes tended to glaze over at the approach of a tedious bore; whilst in his last years in Nairobi, Priscilla reports, *I am afraid the bishop came to dread the sight of him.*

Roland *refused to put voluntary in opposition to stipendiary clergy, since all are in a sense voluntary (as opposed to conscripted).*[7] What he meant by the phrase 'voluntary clergy' were *men in the group, of the group, ordained without giving up their present means of livelihood and giving their services freely.* He emphasized that these persons should be volunteers 'of the group', in that *they would not so much offer themselves as be offered, Ambrose-wise, by their church.*[8]

It cannot be too strongly emphasized that Roland did not mean 'part-time priests' or 'half-time priests'—phrases which caused him to shudder. *A cleric can no more be a half-time cleric than a father can be a half-time father, or a baptized Christian a half-time Christian,* he expostulates.[9] And my father once commented that *He had a great reverence for the priesthood, and he was a priest all the time, awake or asleep.*

I myself recall a discussion with a schoolmate about how much people ought to be paid; I was in the home of my grandparents in Nairobi, arguing with Peter, the eldest son of Canon Bewes of the Church Missionary Society. Granfer, who

---

[7]Priscilla Allen, 'Roland Allen—A Prophet for this Age', *op. cit.,* p. 11.

[8]'A Survey of the Constitution of the Anglican Church in Kenya', *Times of East Africa* (28 April 1932); and Paton, in R.A. Denniston, ed., *Part-Time Priests* (Skeffington & Sons, 1960), p.117.

[9]*The Case for Voluntary Clergy, op. cit.,* p. 89; Canon David Paton failed to appreciate the intensity of Roland's feeling about this, and even allowed the phrase to be used on the dust-cover of the first edition of *The Ministry of the Spirit;* this so horrified Roland's son and daughter that they never thereafter felt able to cooperate with that scholar's further researches.

was also in the room, murmured words to the effect that the Church had a duty to pay its servants properly, but that—*being a priest is not a job. No-one should be paid for being a priest.* My friend and I didn't follow this: it seemed to both of us obvious that being a priest was 'a job'. So Granfer went on: *It is a privilege and a vocation, not a job.* I wasn't at all sure what all these words meant, but Grannie told us not to weary him with questions— and no-one ever argued with Grannie.

Equally disturbing for Roland was the Church's practice of ordaining only callow youths straight out of college:

> *The Apostolic writer did not advise Timothy (nor Titus) to seek for young men . . . He told them to look for men who had already proved that they possessed the qualifications desired, men already married, whose households were such as they ought to be . . . The Apostolic writer wanted men who had experience of the world outside the Christian religious community . . . not 'men of the world' (God forbid!) but men of God in the world.*[10]

By such 'men of God in the world' Roland did not mean what his friend Father Herbert Kelly dubbed *the familiar absurdity of the lay reader.* With approval he cited Kelly's ridicule of the illogicality that the *man who may not celebrate, because he is too uneducated and has not passed examinations, is allowed to preach and minister to souls!*[11]

Although this question of 'voluntary clergy'—of what is nowadays called the 'non-stipendiary ministry'—was a matter of relatively little concern for Roland's non-Anglican colleagues in the Survey Application Trust, *He never had any doubts about what he felt it right to do.*[12]

For much of the 1920s, then, Roland was increasingly concerned with the questions posed by Bishop Azariah in his

---

[10]Article of 29 September 1942 on 'Theological Colleges' submitted to, and rejected by, *The Hibbert Journal.*

[11]*The East & the West*, April 1916, p. 435; cited in '*Sponx*', p. 175.

[12]Alexander McLeish in *The Ministry of the Spirit, op. cit.*, p. xiii.

introduction to 'Sponx'. In 1925 Roland wrote a series of articles on this theme for the Canadian Churchman; and he worked these up, with some material from World Dominion, into a small book called *Voluntary Clergy Overseas*. This was offered to the Oxford University Press, which had published *Pentecost & the World*: it very much impressed the OUP's reader, the novelist Charles Williams, but the publisher himself, Humphrey Milford, over-ruled him.[13]

Roland's Nonconformist colleagues at the World Dominion Press were again unhappy about *Voluntary Clergy Overseas*, so in 1928 he had it privately printed, subtitled *An Answer to the Fifth World Call*. This 'Fifth World Call' was the report of a commission set up by the Missionary Council of the Anglican Church Assembly. As Roland remarks in his preface, it *was a desperate attempt . . . to persuade us that we can supply the need of our people overseas by sending out professional clerics and money from England.*

Roland's 'Answer' was clear and unequivocal:

> *In opposition to all that, I suggest that if we would accept Apostolic guidance, and ordain voluntary clergy, we could meet the whole need everywhere, at home and abroad; and that what is necessary is a complete change of outlook and method.*[14]

In the New Testament, Roland had pointed out several years earlier, *there are two principles enunciated—(1) If any will not work neither shall he eat; and (2) They who serve the altar shall live of the altar. It was the first upon which the primitive Church relied in opposing the payment of clergy . . . It was the second upon which the mediæval Church relied to build up the church order.*[15] This medieval attitude had led to what Thomas Arnold of Rugby eighty years before had called *the overpowering tradition that the ordained ministry was a profession.* It was time, Roland believed, to get

---

[13]See Paton, *Reform of the Ministry, op. cit.,* pp. 87, 91, 93f.

[14]*Voluntary Clergy Overseas* (Amenbury: 1928), Preface.

[15]Letter to *The Church Times,* 14 November 1919.

away from, in Arnold's words: *that pestilent distinction between clergy and laity, which is closely linked to the priestcraft system.*[16]

Because of his exasperation with the Establishment's resistance to the idea of voluntary clergy, Roland has sometimes been accused of wishing to do away with the stipendiary system altogether. But this, Grannie once told me firmly, was not his intention:

> *Surely the word 'condemnation' of prof. clergy was never used by him? . . . the v. fact of V.C. continuing to carry on their profession (tho' some of course one hopes would be retired and experienced men) would make them unable, even if they wished, to carry on the daily tasks of a Vicar of a Parish. Is it not somewhere suggested that a Vicar (or Rector) might, as at present alas, have the nominal charge of several churches and be assisted by 2 or more V. Clergy who would serve the churches the Vicar could not reach, or rarely. Those churches wd then have their regular Communions, the dying visited & 'comforted' . . .* [17]

As Roland once put it: *stipends and salaries are only a convenience and a help in certain cases . . . ministration in holy things is not merely a salaried profession.* It seems likely that he would have agreed with Bishop Lesslie Newbigin's view that: *it may well be that, in certain situations, the 'non-professional' ministry will be seen to be the essential ministry, and that of the full-time professional, the 'auxiliary' or 'supplementary'.*[18] What made Roland sad and annoyed was the reluctance of the hierarchy to confront this issue:

> *'Voluntary Clergy' is not the last resort of the desperate; it enshrines principles of profound truth and importance. The danger in England is that we shall fly to it . . . as a last*

---

[16]J. Fuller & P. Vaughan, *Working for the Kingdom* (SPCK: 1986), p. 170.

[17]Letter of 28th September 1954.

[18]D.M. Paton, ed., *New Forms of Ministry*, Research Pamphlet No. 12 (Edinburgh House: 1965). Three years later the Lambeth Conference agreed with this: *"In some areas the part-time non- stipendiary minister could become the norm"*: (Resolution 33, p. 102).

*resort, in haste and panic, and shall then do wrongly what
we ought to do with forethought and conviction.*[19]

It was misleading, we noted above, to suppose that in
Roland's earlier writings his emphasis on the 'indigenous
Church' was paramount: in fact, this was no more than a 'spin-
off' from his concern for placing total trust in the Holy Spirit. In
just the same way it would be thoroughly misleading to con-
clude that, because in his later writing Roland seems to *concentrate his energies still more narrowly on the single issue of the
voluntary clergy*, therefore the desire for a non-stipendiary ministry was for him a primary objective.[20]

Just as an indigenous Church was vital, in his view, simply
because it could provide an appropriate environment in which
the Holy Spirit could act; so was a non-stipendiary system vital,
not in itself, but simply as an appropriate mechanism to ensure
that a Church could truly *be* a Church—because, in his view: *Any
definition of a Church must include the power to administer the
Sacraments.*[21] A Church which lacked that power for any reason
could not, he maintained, be a genuine Church. By insisting on
restricting the priestly function to an inevitably undermanned
clerical profession, Roland protested, the Anglican Church was
exposing itself to Our Lord's own criticism: 'Ye make the word
of God of none effect by your tradition'.

*What Church founded by the Apostles can we name which
had not its own proper officers and the right and the authority to administer the Sacraments? . . . [In many provinces of*

---

[19]'Money the Foundation of the Church', *The Pilgrim*, 6/4 (July 1926), p. 423.
As Grannie wrote to me: *It will interest you that he said—This is bound to come, only
instead of being accepted (I forget the adverb) it will come of necessity in time of
trouble . . .* One may wonder if recent enormous losses by the Church Commis-
sioners will lead to such 'haste and panic . . . in time of trouble'!

[20]As an example of such a misconception, see, for example, David Paton's
'Biographical & Theological Essay' at the beginning of *Reform of the Ministry*,
p. 19f.

[21]'The "Nevius Method" in Korea', *World Dominion*, July 1930, p. 13.

the Anglican Church] the Sacraments of Christ are occa-
sional luxuries . . . Where in the Bible can we find such a
thing? Where in the early Church? . . . it is impossible to
maintain a tradition in a Church which keeps an open Bible,
and not to face the obligation which that open Bible lays
upon them.[22]

Recently Åke Talltorp, a Swedish Lutheran, has helpfully
emphasized this fundamental aspect of Granfer's thinking:

Roland Allen in his writings clearly and frequently empha-
sizes the necessity of the sacramental life as the foundation of
the mission of the Church. The eucharistic experience is to
Allen a necessary consequence of the baptism. The frequent
celebration of the eucharist as a corporate act of worship is
regarded as the normal pattern in the local Church. This
sacramental dimension was to him a matter of course, and a
condition necessary for the growth and expansion of the
Church in mission.[23]

This insight, together with Harry Boer's, mentioned in
Chapters VIII and IX accounts for many of the apparent anoma-
lies of Roland's teaching, and incidentally goes far to explain
why it is so difficult to pin him down into any category—so that
we read such comments as, that *the Anglo-Catholic Allen so*
modifies his episcopal views in the light of his belief in the power of the
Holy Spirit in the young Church that they are very close to Congrega-
tionalism.[24]

---

[22]See 'The Church & an Itinerant Ministry', *The East & the West*, 25/98 (April
1927); and *The Case for Voluntary Clergy, op. cit.*, p. 25. Mark 7:13 is cited at the
beginning of Roland's Preface to the latter work.

[23]Talltorp, *op. cit.*, p . 67.

[24]P. Beyerhaus & H. Lefever, *The Responsible Church* (World Dominion
Press, 1964), p. 55.

'the most distinguished of the brothers during his lifetime'
the Ven. Willoughby C. Allen,
Archdeacon of Manchester, c. 1909

CHAPTER XI

Travelling Salesman

'the laying of the foundation stone of a hospital and school'
Murhu, India, 1910

In his introduction to *The Spontaneous Expansion of the Church and the Causes which hinder it*, V.S. Azariah, the Bishop of Dornakal, identified some of the awkward questions which Roland was posing the Church in that book—as he had been doing in earlier writings. Among the ones the Bishop mentions, we may note particularly in the present context: *Is it not true that by employing a paid army of evangelists, the task of evangelization is shifted from the Church to a paid agency?* Or again: *In how many Churches is the Apostolic rule of weekly 'Breaking of Bread' being followed?* or *We accept a short training for a teacher, and demand a long training for a man who is to celebrate the Eucharist. Why do we do this?* and *Why do we not employ voluntary workers far more widely?*

129

These questions and similar ones had been exercising Roland's mind for a long time. He was writing in the Church Times on the subject as early as 1919. A letter from him in the Daily Telegraph in 1922 gave rise to two more or less sympathetic leading articles. And an earlier one in The Churchman elicited a laudatory endorsement from Bishop Robert Paddock of Eastern Oregon, who claimed that by adopting Roland's principles *our own Church has grown faster than almost anywhere else in the United States*. The following year SPCK published the first of several longer treatises by Roland on the same theme— a booklet entitled *Voluntary Clergy;* and he noted examples of such clergy being ordained in southern Ohio and in New Jersey.[1] And then, as mentioned earlier, in the summer and autumn of 1924 he crossed the Atlantic, to investigate the failure of a scheme known as the Archbishops' Western Canada Fund (AWCF).

The objectives of AWCF, when it was launched in 1910, with ideas drawn both from the South Africa Church Railway Mission and from the Australian Bush Brotherhood, were to provide men and money from England for Anglican churches in western Canada during a ten-year period, after which time it was anticipated that the churches would be self-supporting and the fund could be closed. This had not happened. Roland sought to discover why this was so.

I went out at the end of May, he tells us in the first of a series of nine articles about this project, *and travelled to the Pacific and back by different routes to see what a visitor could see of the real state of the Church there.* Exasperatingly for any biographer seeking to describe his life and travels, he then goes on to remark that: *I do not propose to describe my journey, still less the people whom I met.*[2] However, we know that he spent some time in each of the areas

---

[1]Letter to *The Church Times,* 7 September 1923: see also e.g. *The Living Church,* 7 July 1923 and 1 November 1924.

[2]*The Canadian Churchman,* 4 June 1925, p. 362.

served by the Fund—the dioceses of Athabasca, Calgary, Edmonton, Qu'Appelle, and Saskatoon.

It was at first his intention to write a history of the AWCF for publication. But what he observed decided him against any such endeavour: *The history would be too personal,* he wrote to Archdeacon Knowles of Qu'Appelle diocese, *& I shrink from mentioning names while people are still alive.*[3]

Many commentators had suggested that the failure of AWCF was simply an effect of the First World War; but Roland argued cogently that this was a misconception. *He is quite right,* comments a Canadian historian, *because it was obvious by 1913 that the missions had fallen far short of the mark anticipated in terms of finance and manpower. The war dealt a death blow to the work and provided a convenient excuse for the collapse of the mission.*[4]

The scheme had worked only where three conditions prevailed: a growing population in a definite place; a resident priest; and a congregation that became strong enough to maintain that priest. Otherwise AWCF had not worked—and in Roland's opinion it *could* not have worked—because it was in practice unrealistically dependent on an endless and growing supply of 'professional' priests, trained in theological colleges, and earning stipends:

> *I said to one of the Bishops in Canada, 'You sell Christ's grace. You say to men, If you will subscribe so many dollars, you shall have the ministration of a student. If you subscribe so many more, you shall have a deacon. If you provide so many more you shall have a priest, as soon as I have one to send you . . .' He answered me, 'That is crudely expressed, but it is crudely true'.*

Roland pointed out that the closing report of the AWCF *while it tells us that 70 churches have been built and 168 sites*

---

[3]Letter from 'Amenbury', dated 10th February 1926, which concludes: *My meeting with you was the brightest spot in my tour.*

[4]David J. Carter, 'The Railway Mission–Regina', *Journal of the Canadian Church Historical Society*, X/4 (December 1968), pp. 212f.

purchased, also tells us that help has been given to 7 candidates in training for Holy Orders. 168: 70: 7: that is the proportion. This, he maintained, was a preposterous state of affairs; what then could be done? *The diaconate is not what the Church needs; she needs priests.* Nor were itinerant priests an adequate answer:

> *A system which makes the regular service of a congregation depend upon an itinerant priest is not only unapostolic, but also bad in itself . . . That the Church in Canada has many excellent itinerating priests whose sense of the needs of the country keeps them hard at work year after year is indeed inspiring and a cause for thanksgiving, but that does not alter the fact that the system is a bad system . . .*

So Roland terminated his brief official memorandum to the Archbishops with the following conclusion:

> *This is the lesson which, I would urge, is taught us by the history of the AWCF. We can either send out men who will act as parochial clergy and hold services for groups of people; or we can send out men to establish churches on a self-supporting basis from the very beginning . . . If we do the second the missioners must be able to pass on, leaving churches (not necessarily buildings) established and settled behind them . . . [They] must be authorised to appeal, not so much for money, as for service, and to look for suitable men to be ordained in every place, who may minister to their fellows, free, gratis, and for nothing. In other words the stipendiary system must be subordinated to the spiritual needs of the church . . .*

> *We cannot staff the world with paid clergy,*
> he expostulates in his letter to Archdeacon Knowles,
> *We shall have to 'think again', and think not in terms of 'see houses' and cathedrals, stipendiaries, money & men, but in terms of souls.*

The experience gained by him in this particular 'survey' confirmed Roland's dedication to what his daughter identified as the 'third theme in the fugue' of his life: that is to say, whether lack of faith in the Holy Spirit were not seriously damaging the ministry of the Church; not merely in Canada, but throughout the Anglican communion: *We put the maintenance of a paid clergy before the commands of Christ, and we get Church members who, when separated from their paid clerical nurses, are as helpless as babies.*[5]

Roland's tour in Canada was followed by two more such oversea visits, paid for by the Survey Application Trust, notwithstanding Cochrane's doubts whether the work undertaken was really relevant to the Trust's objectives. In the course of each of these expeditions—to South Africa and Rhodesia in 1926 and to southern India and Assam in 1927/28—Roland resolved to make it his principal task to attempt to 'sell' to the local Anglican bishops, clergy and layfolk his ideas about the non-stipendiary ministry.

As so often, it is necessary for his biographer to resort to detective work to identify details of these travels. We can only be sure that Beatrice was with him in Rhodesia, for example, because he used for some of his notes an envelope addressed to her in that country. He started by basing himself at St. Faith's, Rusapi, to help Canon Edgar Lloyd. We know that he was in Umtata in October 1926, because he wrote a letter from the Royal Hotel there. We know he was in Pretoria ten days' later, because he addressed the diocesan synod. But his reports and diaries about these travels tend to be singularly uninformative on everyday topics; in a characteristic letter from Assam he remarks to his son:

> *I am not sending any diary this week. I had an interesting & pleasing ride on an elephant into the jungle & a view of another tea-garden in the making, but that is not the sort of stuff that I want to put in a diary.*

Nothing short of painstaking field research in each of the countries he visited could elicit a really clear picture of what he did, and where.

---

[5]Letter in *The Record*, 29 May 1924.

What concerned him was to try to communicate as forcefully as possible his message about the need for voluntary clergy. And when he felt the occasion demanded it, Roland's *quiet voice* was raised in true prophetic admonition. Addressing Pretoria's diocesan synod, he departed from his usual practice, and read from a prepared text, explaining that he was anxious to use no word that he had not meditated on and prayed over:

> *I admire you and respect you,* he assured his audience, *I could speak long in praise of your faith and love . . . I am not here to set forth any original ideas of my own. I simply appeal from a modern tradition to the teaching and practice of Christ and His Apostles . . . unless you can show that I misrepresent [their] thinking . . . you are criticizing not me, but them . . .* Nor would it do for them to protest that times had changed since the time of Christ and His Apostles: *The application of principles may change as years pass, but principles do not change, and I am going to confine myself closely to principles tonight.*

He then carefully rehearsed many arguments in favour of voluntary clergy in circumstances like those in South Africa. *In many places today the choice is not between voluntary clergy and stipendiary clergy, but between voluntary clergy and none. I deal with voluntary clergy simply because I do not see how we can establish the Church without voluntary clergy. My real subject is therefore not Voluntary Clergy, but the Establishment of the Church.*

As he had remarked elsewhere, *I have no desire that what men call 'my' remedy should be adopted. It is not in any true sense 'mine'; but it is the only one which I can imagine, and it has the advantage of catholic antiquity. Still I do not want men to accept it, if they know of a better remedy.*[6]

The body of his address in Pretoria was later reprinted in the missiological journal The East & the West.[7] But that article does

---

[6]Letter to Principal of Bishop's College, Cheshunt (2 November 1923).
[7]'The Church & an Itinerant Ministry', *op.cit.*, pp. 123-133.

not include Roland's introductory remarks, still less his ringing peroration:

> *My Lord Bishop, my brethren of the clergy and of the laity, I have done. We are now met before the throne of the Most High God our Father, before the judgement seat of Christ, in the presence of the Holy Ghost, our teacher and sanctifier.*
>
> *Solemnly here I beg you to repent:*
>
> *[1] You are preaching and practising, and by connivance and toleration accepting a denial of Christ's Gospel of 'Rise up and walk in the grace and power of the Lord'—by teaching men to wait till you can do something for them yourselves;*
>
> *[2] You are starving the children of God committed to your care, and leaving them a defenceless prey to charlatans and quacks;*
>
> *[3] You are subordinating Christ's commands, Christ's Sacraments, to money, in that you say 'We must have money before we can constitute the Church'.*
>
> *Again I say, solemnly in the Name of Christ I beseech you to repent; and I beseech you to repent and amend now, at once. Do not delay for an hour. Is not that how you preach to others? Do you not say to them: 'Delay not to amend. Do not put off the day of salvation'? The children of Christ are now suffering all those ills which I have enumerated, and many others. Do not then delay to repent. Repent now, and amend your practice today. Souls are perishing while you debate. In the Name of Christ. Amen.*[8]

Truly, the members of the Synod must have been wondering whether an Amos or a John the Baptist were come to Pretoria! Afterwards Roland felt obliged to write a slightly

---

[8]Address to Diocesan Synod of Pretoria, 26th October 1926. manuscript note.

135

penitent letter to the Bishop, whose motive in inviting him to speak to the Synod had evidently been based on the assumption that his visitor planned simply to outline a practical expedient, a methodology which might help the Church in South Africa to diminish staff shortages; instead, the Synod found itself confronted by a passionate crusader with a burning sense of mission.

Although a largely favourable debate followed this address, nothing much happened in consequence of it whilst Roland was still in southern Africa. A couple of years later, however, a letter in The Canadian Churchman from Roland's admirer, Frederick Junkison, is headed 'Voluntary Clergy in Capetown'.[9] In this is summarised *a few details of the proceedings of the Capetown Synod, South Africa, as reported in the Church Chronicle of October 25th, last.* It appears that the Coadjutor Bishop of Capetown, Dr. J.O. Nash, moved: *That this Synod approves the principle of ordaining suitable men engaged in various occupations as unpaid clergy to supplement the regular clergy and to minister to small congregations.* After an interesting debate the word *approves* was deleted, and the words *commends to the Bishops the further study of* substituted. The amended motion was carried by about 70 to 12 in the House of Clergy, and almost unanimously in the House of Laymen.

Junkison comments that *The debate, if not inspired by, revolved round the book 'Voluntary Clergy Overseas' by the Rev. Roland Allen.* Apart from some of Bishop Nash's remarks, the writer quotes at length from the favourable speech by the Rev. R.H.C. Birt, Principal of Diocesan College, Rondebosch, which clearly demonstrates how Roland's ideas were in certain influential quarters beginning to have some effect:

> *Surely there are many elderly men who would be most excellent people to minister, as priests, to out-of-the-way congregations. Is it not true that a large section of the*

---

[9]Letter dated 28 November 1928.

*laymen consider the clergy far removed from themselves? . . .
If we were to draw a line down the middle of this house (the
Synod) we should find on one side men, who if they were not
efficient in their jobs would be unemployed; and on the other
side we should find men (the clergy) who even if they were
not efficient would not lose their jobs. That makes a good deal
of difference to the outlook of the layman on the clergy and
the outlook of the clergy on life as a whole. The clergy have
never been up against the real things of life which the
layman has to face. If we can bridge that gulf we will help the
Church enormously, and one thing would be to have men
who as ministers are earning their living at other things.*

In India Roland started out by accepting an invitation from
his friend, the first Indian bishop in the Anglican Church,
Vedanayakam Samuel Azariah of Dornakal, to speak to his
Clergy School for up to one-and-a-half hours a day from Mon-
day to Saturday, during a fortnight shortly before Christmas
1927. Roland's diary makes a few, tantalizingly sketchy, references to his appreciation of his surroundings—the railway
journey up the Ghat to Poona, for example, a 'drama' of Jeremiah
performed by the divinity students, the *fireflies twinkling in the
trees and on the grass in the compound* . . . Even more tantalizingly
he remarks on *A quiet day spent in writing up some notes on South
Indian Union, which I tore up.* But generally the diary is exclu-
sively concerned with the transmission of his message, and its
reception.[10]

The same applies when he travels north, to take up an
invitation from George Clay Hubback, then Bishop of Assam,
with whom he had been keeping up a trenchant correspondence
about voluntary clergy during the preceding two years. During
a half-hour trip in a dugout canoe and as long again in a steam

---

[10]The early part of his diary, and his intense correspondence with Bishop
Hubback, are reprinted in Paton, *Reform of the Ministry, op. cit.*, pp. 106-164. The
rest of the diary exists only in faded manuscript carbon copies in the Rhodes
House collection.

launch: *The view of the Hills from the River (and from the Wrights' bungalow) was enchanting. But that is not business for this diary.* Nor, except in barest outline, is an account of his having to jump head first into a moving train, with his bags flung in after him. It is just possible from the diary to work out details of his two-month-long itinerary in Assam and Bengal, and to identify most of the persons he met: but nearly all the entries concentrate on his attempts to communicate his message, and its reception by—one suspects—the somewhat bemused tea planters, oil engineers, civil servants, and their wives, and sundry Indian clergy and members of the Oxford Mission to Calcutta to whom Roland addressed himself.

When Roland first arrived in Assam the Bishop suggested that he should try to stay long enough to address the Bishops' Conference in Calcutta. But Roland anticipated a repetition of his *faux pas* in Pretoria: *I told him that I doubted whether they would wish to hear me, and that if I did I should call them to repentance. He was very grave at that . . . he is thinking, and I do not spare him.*

Roland was much encouraged by the reaction of many of the lay persons he met: *wherever I go I find people ready, almost eager, for Vol.Cler.* But bitter disappointment was in store, for this Bishop was to prove too timid to undertake the pioneering experiment his visitor so forcefully urged upon him: *I am not prepared to follow out your advice to ordain men, untrained and unprepared, to take up the most difficult work of the Sacred Ministry.* As Roland remarked in his diary: *The moment that the Bishop or anyone else sets up a kind of ideal standard, he instantly and inevitably feels that he cannot take the risk of ordaining anyone. The Theological College delivers them from applying any criterion except the one 'He has been through the set course'. That closes the question of 'fitness' for them.*

With this disappointment Roland had virtually reached the end of his active career. In one of his last letters to Bishop Hubback he tries to cheer himself up by summarizing what small successes he did appear to have had:

In spite of all my failures, I see that men are beginning to think seriously. Missionary Methods *has exercised and is exercising some influence (more perhaps outside my own Church than inside), and the idea of voluntary clergy is gaining ground . . . It is not all failure . . . Whether it is through my lips or through the lips of others, men are hearing the Saviour pleading and one day I believe and hope they will act.*

But what has been called *The greatest achievement—and the greatest disappointment—in Allen's life* [11] was yet to come.

---

[11]Patrick Vaughan in Fuller & Vaughan, *op. cit.*, p. 172.

Standing:
Priscilla, Iohn and Elizabeth Brooke Mallaby.
Seated:
Winkie holding Edith,
Beatrice with Hubert, Roland.
Nairobi, 1934

CHAPTER XII

The Case for Voluntary Clergy

'his wonderful eyes just a sapphire blaze'

Although disappointed by its reception in Canada, India and South Africa, Roland longed to carry his message wider still. He corresponded with his wife's cousin, one of the Tarleton family, a priest from the Anglican Province of Sydney, retired to

Tasmania. He wrote to Bishop Llewellyn Gwynne of Cairo of plans to pay an extended visit to Iohn in the Sudan during the winter of 1928/1929, and the Bishop suggested that he might be able to act as a relief chaplain in Upper Egypt. Most of all, Roland would have liked to cross the Atlantic again, to visit Canada's huge southern neighbour:

> *I was shy of thrusting myself upon your attention,* he wrote in reply to a friendly letter from one Bishop Sanford in the USA. *I am constantly dreaming of a day when I may possibly visit the States and study my problem there; but I have done so much wandering like a lost dog, thrusting myself upon people, that I have grown to shrink from it more than ever.*[1]

The problem, however, as Roland stressed, was not simply one for the overseas mission field—although there, of course, in the gigantic dioceses and 'chaplaincies' of such places as Canada and tropical Africa, it could appear in starkest form. The problem was equally dramatic when rural parishes in England were reduced to *a mere fragment of a church in some larger area . . . Everything, the life of the Church, the Sacraments, everything is to be subordinated to money . . . Who cares what they think? They have no money. Having souls does not matter.*[2]

> *We ought to recognise that the ministry of Christ and the Sacraments of Christ are the foundations, not the coping stones, of a Church . . . We cannot build securely on any foundation but that laid by Christ and His Apostles . . . Did not Christ say 'Where two or three', and shall we put Him right and say Yes, if they can afford to support a stipendiary cleric?*[3]

He was horrified by the distortion wrought by the Church's constant need for money to support the stipendiary system: *to*

---

[1] Letter dated 26 August 1930.
[2] Letter on 'Church Revenues Report' in *The Guardian*, 30 April 1924.
[3] 'The Church & an Itinerant Ministry', *op. cit.*, pp. 127, 131.

build upon money is to build on a foundation that is not of the Gospel; it is to bind the Church to the chariot wheels of Mammon.[4]

He recognised, of course, that what he was proposing demanded enormous changes of attitude, both among clergy and laity: *I do not think that we can change our ideas and their ideas in a day . . . The Apostles could go into places like the cities (villages we should call them) of Asia Minor, Greece and Crete, and establish Churches, and ordain clergy. Our people are not worse than those people . . . Some people in Canada told me that the men could not be found there. I know that it is false . . . But the difficulty of a long tradition stays with us. I do not minimize it, but I do say that it should be broken.*

We have to adjust our minds to a conception which is very unfamiliar . . . if we think of voluntary clergy as doing the work of the present stipendiary clergy in their familiar way, we at once get into difficulties.

(1) We have to think of qualifications as the writer of the Epistle to Timothy thought of them, and that is very strange to us.

(2) We have to think of the ministry as given to the Church rather than to the individual ordinand, and that is strange to us. We give a Church, a 'sphere', to a priest, rather than a ministry to a Church . . .

(4) We think almost entirely in terms of one man one parish: one priest-in-charge assisted possibly by others: we have to learn to think in terms of a college of priests in very small Churches . . . &c

And so, in a valiant final effort to bring home to the Establishment the importance of his thesis, Roland sent a copy of *Voluntary Clergy Overseas* to every one of the Anglican bishops, who were to be attending the 1930 Lambeth Conference, with an

---

[4]'Money the Foundation of the Church', *op. cit.,* p. 428.

143

individually signed covering letter (Appendix 4). Several of them responded warmly. His old ally, Bishop Henry Whitehead of Madras, for example, was moved to protest:

> But why is it printed privately and not given the widest possible circulation? It ought to be broadcasted and read by all the bishops, archdeacons, parish priests, parish council-lors, communicants and earnest churchmen and church-women throughout the Anglican Communion . . . [5]

Partly in consequence of Roland's work, an authoritative Provisional Committee for Voluntary Clergy was established under the chairmanship of the Bishop of Middleton, and sent a forceful statement to each member of the National Assembly of the Church of England. This commended Roland's proposals for full consideration by the Lambeth Conference. It ended forthrightly:

> In conclusion, let us state that we do not bring forward this suggestion as a palliative for present evils, but as a change which is good in itself, and will do much to deepen Spiritual Life throughout the Church.[6]

In consequence of this last effort of Roland's, the matter of voluntary clergy did indeed get onto the Lambeth agenda. But the meagre outcome was a bitter disappointment for him: a mere statement that the conference *sees no insuperable objection to the ordination, with provincial sanction and under proper safeguards, where the need is great, of such Auxiliary Priests.*

In fact, as subsequent history has shown, Roland had not vainly cast his bread upon the waters. His ideas about voluntary clergy were taken up with enthusiasm by F.R. Barry, then Vicar of Oxford's University Church, and later to become Bishop of Southwell, who seems to have given currency to the more precise term 'non-stipendiary', and who emphasized that the

---

[5]Letters cited in *Reform of the Ministry, op. cit.,* pp. 120ff and p. 95.
[6]See e.g. *The Guardian,* 8th February, 1929.

system would *help to preserve Christianity from becoming a carica-
ture of itself, as something people do after working hours.*[7] And
gradually, over the years, Roland's basic premises have become
more and more widely accepted, not least overseas: the Chinese
Church altered its Canons as early as 1934, and ten years after
Roland's death no fewer than 43 percent of the Anglican clergy
in the Hong Kong diocese were in secular employment. More
recently similar developments have taken place in Tanzania
and Singapore, Ecuador and Nicaragua, the USA and—as he
would doubtless have been delighted to know—in Canada's
Keewatin province.

But most of this was hidden from Roland: and much time in
his declining years was spent in profound depression—a problem that had in any case always tended to dog him, being (in his
daughter's view) *a typical cyclothymic; but I remember his saying to
me that there was no need to be depressed because (I do not remember
the exact words) he was on the winning side (or something to that
effect).*[8]

In *Voluntary Clergy Overseas*, as in most of his books, Roland
made sure that neither the Bishops nor anyone else could plead
lack of time to consider his arguments. Not only is the book itself
brief and its language crystal clear, but he prefaces it with an
Analysis, setting out in a few pungent phrases the thrust and
content of each chapter.

These elaborations of the list of contents to provide such
summaries were a feature of almost all his books. These and the
index were usually the product of a combined effort by his
family: he, Priscilla, and Iohn would sit round together, arguing
how best to express key concepts in the fewest possible words.
Iohn remembered the almost mischievous glee with which they
would compose index entries like these:

[7]*The Relevance of the Church* (Nisbet, 1935), Ch. 6.
[8]'Roland Allen: a Prophet for this Age', *op. cit.*, p. 9.

CLERGY:	a luxury,
	strangers to the congregation,
	autocrats, . . .
LAITY:	earnestness of,
	humiliation of,
	ignorance imputed to,
	impotence of,
	indifference of,
	liberality of,
	stinginess of, . . . &c

Beatrice, who was very much a late Victorian lady, with a relatively ill-developed sense of humour, tended to be rather taken aback by such evidence of frivolity in her family. A nephew recalls, for example, 'Aunt B's' disapproval of Roland's nickname—'Beelzebub'—for the coke stove at Amenbury, and her reproachful expostulations whenever her husband got up from the dining table, saying cheerfully *I must go and poke Bub . . .*

The above examples of indexing are taken from Roland's last major book, which, as Priscilla recounts, *was written with immense care and was published by a different publisher, who used better paper and print, so that it was altogether a fine book. It was a great disappointment to us all when it failed to sell or make much impression.*[9] The trouble was, as Bishop Azariah himself had commented soothingly a few years before: *The Church which is accustomed to the rule of 'University graduates', 'Latin learning' and 'a Title to a Living' will not change in a day!* [10]

The Case for Voluntary Clergy brought together and elaborated all Roland's principal arguments on this theme, at home and overseas. It has in more recent years been summarized, in *The Ministry of the Spirit*: but, as with *Pentecost & the World* in the same collection, the mordant subtlety of Roland's summaries

---

[9]*Ibid.*, p. 11.

[10]Letter from the Bishop of Dornakal, 29th December 1923.

and indices has had to be sacrificed to the space available in an anthology.

Attention is drawn to these details, because what Lesslie Newbigin has described as *this quiet voice* was by no means always so quiet and deceptively gentle, especially when it came to actual face-to-face discussion. One reason that Roland's work was not given a more receptive hearing in his lifetime was very probably his own fault. As he remarked in a letter to the Bishop of Nyasaland:

I personally incline to value written words above spoken. In writing I can weigh my words and destroy any that upon reconsideration I do not wholly approve. When I talk I am always in danger of speaking on the spur of the moment words which I afterwards regret. I take too much for granted, I press my point too hard for my hearer, I hurry, I interrupt him. In writing I cannot do that . . . [11]

And he had another reason for preferring writing to talking:

If I speak I am always afraid that I may disturb someone's faith, and I hate that sort of negative effect . . . When I talk I have never found any difficulty in answering objections raised . . . but I did it furiously and almost as much against myself as against my interlocutor, because I did not like doing it at all. I hated the feeling that I was destroying something valuable, even if weak.[12]

His nephew's recollection of such belligerent conduct, even when talking to a schoolboy, has been recorded above. One of Iohn's school-friends recalls that when someone expressed views with which Roland disagreed he could appear to be *a dedicated fanatic—his wonderful eyes just a sapphire blaze.* Even in writing, Roland was often consciously stern:

If my voice sounds harsh in your ears, my tone disrespectful, try to believe that I have been driven to the conviction that

---

[11]Letter of 1st November 1929.
[12]*Reform of the Ministry, op. cit.,* p.191.

*this is no time for mincing words. And excuse me when I beg
you to face the question before us and to say Yea or Nay, for
there is no room here for Perhaps, or Possibly, or To a certain
degree, or any other qualification, nor is there room for a
polite acquiescence which means nothing. Forgive me.*[13]

When the Bishop of Assam, George Hubback, of whom
Roland comments in his diary that *he is so good and gentle*,
complained that *you are a little hard on us bishops*, Roland replied:
*Of course I am ... bishops know quite well that England cannot
supply all the world with clergy ... If, when I point out that the only
inexhaustible supply is on the field, men tell me either that it is not
there, or not there in a form in which they can draw from it. I naturally
ask whether they have tried, and how they know? I suppose that is too
hard ...* In consequence of his vehemence, Roland tended often
to arouse defensive hostility, when all he really sought was
rational discussion. Bishop Hubback frequently took him to
task about this with some exasperation:

*You have neither sympathy nor use for a man who cannot at
once go the whole of the journey that you have taken a
lifetime to tread ... You do not give people the impression of
a man with a message from Our Lord. If you have one, as
you believe ... then you must show more of Christ's spirit in
your dealings with people. Love, I know, has to speak hard
words, but they are words that hurt to heal. Your words too
often hurt without healing.*

And the Bishop goes on to cite *two very different people who on
the whole were very sympathetic to your message*:

1.   *'I entirely agree with Mr. Allen's proposals, but he
himself is the worst possible exponent of them.'*

2.   *'Mr. Allen seems to disapprove of everybody in the
world except his own family.'*

It did not help, of course, that those Roland was addressing

---

[13]Letter to the Principal of Bishop's College, Cheshunt, 2 November 1923.

could often, if only subconsciously, react to this unencumbered outsider by thinking: *What can he understand of our problems, this man who bears not the burden and heat of the day?* And indeed he was apt to overlook genuine pastoral constraints, such as the reluctance of most laity to consider rising to the challenges his ideas posed: *They were emphatic that they would rather have a monthly celebration from what we may call a professional padre than more frequent ones from a man chosen from among themselves,* writes Bishop Hubback. What is more, Roland was easily deceived by people's politeness into assuming that they fully agreed with him. But as the Bishop remarks of some of the planters Roland had been talking to in Assam, they *told me that except on the night when you were there, there had been no mention of or talk about your proposals . . . They were quite clear that the time was not ripe.*[14]

A problem of a different kind was expressed to Roland by the Rev. Chakrabarti, the Indian vicar of St. Mary's, Calcutta, who:

> *had read 'Sponx' and evidently agreed with it; but he said 'We can do nothing with English Bishops in the position of Metropolitan; we can make no progress, but if I say anything they will think that I want to be made a Bishop'.*

Another difficulty, perhaps, was the fact that it was not very comfortable for many of his critics to feel some twinges of conscience. As an editorial in the *Norwich Diocesan Gazette* remarked of *The Case for Voluntary Clergy:*

> *We consider that the author's position is unassailable. But what a nuisance he is! He makes one feel thoroughly ashamed, and incidentally he shows up the worldliness of the Church—a worldliness that affects most of us.*[15]

---

[14]Letters (March 7 and May 17, 1928) cited in *Reform of the Ministry, op. cit.,* pp. 154ff.

[15]April 1930.

Roland's distaste for compromise, too, was distinctly un-Anglican: *Uncle R. seemed to be rather one-track minded*, complained his nephew; *he would talk the hind leg off a donkey without change of subject*.[16] But others have seen this as a strength:

> *Allen's primary value lies (as is being increasingly seen today) precisely in the area which, one feels, most irritated the Church leaders of his own day: the raising with ruthless persistence of precisely those theological issues which are most easily evaded because they call into question current practice.*[17]

---

[16]R.M. Allen, *Notes for a Life of Willoughby Charles Allen* (1975), p. 34.
[17]Paton, *Reform of the Ministry, op. cit.*, p. 43.

CHAPTER XIII

East Africa

'members of his own family'
Priscilla, Beatrice & Iohn at Mwanza in 1957

As we noted earlier, one critic in Assam considered that *Mr. Allen seems to disapprove of everybody in the world except his own family.* A principal reason for this approval of members of his own family was their direct personal involvement, and commitment to the principles which Roland propounded. Perhaps the most conspicuous example of this was displayed by Iohn (my father) after he graduated in 1927.

As early as 1924 Roland had written to Bishop Azariah about Iohn:

> *He is now at college. There is a missionary in spirit. But I tell him not to join a paid professional order. He is a man with all the priestly characteristics; and I say, earn your own living, not by using the priesthood as a means of getting a living . . .*[1]

Iohn left college with the deliberate intention of finding work in a suitable capacity for one of his father's proposed 'voluntary clergy overseas'. With this objective he joined the Sudan Plantations Syndicate, then engaged in establishing the renowned 'Gezira Scheme', designed to cultivate cotton and other crops on a massive irrigated area between the White and the Blue Niles in what was then the 'Anglo-Egyptian Condominium' of the Sudan.

In this context, Iohn found himself led to put into practice yet another controversial idea that Roland had begun to articulate, but which he did not expound until two years later, in an article which the editor of the Church Quarterly Review refused to publish, being apprehensive at the time of *a schism in the Church of England*.[2]

Iohn was posted by the Syndicate to remote places, where he was often far from any 'professional' clergy, and usually completely on his own as a Christian: so if he were to receive the Sacrament of Holy Communion he could do so only by the expedient of celebrating himself, as a layman. With some misgivings, he did this (and it seems that the local Anglican Bishop, Llewellyn Gwynne, whom Iohn visited and told about it, did not categorically disapprove).

---

[1] Letter to the Bishop of Dornakal, 30 January 1924.

[2] Letter to Roland from Canon Maynard Smith, 5th January 1930.

Most of Iohn's interesting journal, kept during this experiment, has been preserved: but for our present purposes it is enough to note the rigorous arguments in Roland's letters, in response to some of Iohn's questions, which demonstrate him 'thinking aloud' when his mind was still clearly at the height of its powers (Appendix 3).

This experience in the Sudan gave Iohn an opportunity to meet and talk with some Muslim divines and scholars, giving him a respect for their integrity and learning which he was later to communicate to his father. One episode is characteristic. The local manager for the Syndicate had occasion to send Iohn out to recruit labourers for the cotton scheme: aware of Iohn's deep Christian convictions, he gave him a warning: *Mind you keep off religion. The local bigwig is a fanatical Muslim.*

When Iohn arrived this potentate greeted him with the traditional words: *There is no God but God, and Muhammad is the Prophet of God. There is no God but God,* agreed Iohn politely, *and Jesus Christ is His Son. Blasphemy!* exclaimed his host and, dismissing his underlings to deal with the matter of recruitment, called Iohn into his home for a long day's theological argument—a discussion that was frequently renewed, since the 'bigwig' made it known to the mystified syndicate manager that this learned Christian would be favoured whenever it was necessary to recruit labour in that area.

Roland hoped to visit Iohn in the Sudan, but was unable to arrange this on his way to Assam or on the return journey. He was planning to do so during the second winter of Iohn's sojourn there: but after less than two years, to the great disappointment of both his parents, Iohn made up his mind that he would never be able to work contentedly in commerce. Instead, he enrolled in Britain's Colonial Education Service and went out as a schoolmaster to what was then the League of Nations' Trust Territory of Tanganyika.[3]

---

[3]This was the erstwhile German East Africa, today the mainland part of the United Republic of Tanzania.

In 1930 Roland's one-time Latin pupil, Winifred Brooke (now herself a well qualified teacher) followed Iohn out to marry him, in Tanga, the main seaport for northern Tanganyika, where she herself started the town's first school for girls. Roland and Beatrice visited them there at the end of the year. Their daughter, Priscilla, also came out to help her sister-in-law, and then joined the staff of the Macmillan Memorial Library in Nairobi, in the neighbouring Kenya Colony.

Roland and Beatrice decided that in order to be reasonably close to both their children they, too, would leave England for good, and settle down in the healthy climate and inexpensive environment of Nairobi. They returned to England to pack away their unwanted furniture and other items from Amenbury, and Roland briefly relieved his brother Willoughby at Saham Toney in Norfolk, where he was now Rector.

By the end of 1931 they were back in Tanga, to be on hand to help Winkie after their first grandchild was born on St. Stephen's Day. Thereafter they remained in East Africa, apart from one more trip to the British Isles in 1936-37, which included visits to Beatrice's sister Edith in Weybridge, and to Jersey in the Channel Islands, where Winkie and her children were staying with her mother and sister, during and after Iohn's home leave.

Iohn used to remark that it is misleading to suggest that Granfer 'decided to settle' in East Africa: *He never really intended to settle anywhere. I think that he found that his travelling days were done, and simply stopped where he happened to be. Everywhere in the world he was at home, so it did not matter where he actually was.*[4]

Apart from her war service in Britain and the Middle East, Priscilla was also to make her home in East Africa for the rest of her life. She continued to be her parents' constant companion until her mother's death in 1960. Since she never married, Iohn and Winkie's son and daughters were Roland's and Beatrice's only grandchildren.

---

[4]See Hans Wolfgang Metzger, *Roland Allen* (Gütersloh: Gütersloher Verlangshaus Gerd Mohn, 1970), pp. 58f. [footnote].

Soon after his arrival in Nairobi Roland carried out a 'Survey of the Constitution of the Anglican Church in Kenya'. In a commentary on this he returned once again to his theme:

> *The choice in this case is not between stipendiary clerics and voluntary clerics, but between voluntary clerics and none. We can follow the Apostolic rule and establish Churches freely, or we can subordinate the Church and the Commands of Christ to the stipendiary tradition.*[5]

When Roland first arrived in East Africa he used sometimes to be invited to preach. On 1st May, 1932, in particular, he preached a notable sermon in Nairobi's All Saints' Cathedral, and again on Palm Sunday in 1937. But his unorthodox views were disturbing in a very conventional missionary environment. During his Michaelmas sermon in 1935, for example, his exhortation to the settler congregation was startling:

> *Sooner or later many of you, and your children, will go up-country. There, Sunday after Sunday, you will have no Church to go to. You know that. Well then, what are you going to do? . . . Will you say . . . the Church is here where I am, and if there is no Chaplain here, I am here a King and Priest unto God, for myself, for my household, for my neighbours . . . that is fighting a battle on Christ's behalf against the sloth which says 'If there is no Chaplain to do things for us, we can do nothing, but hold a dance, or a tennis tournament' . . . You have the secret. You know what is the Christian fight, and that you are fighting it, and that Michael and all his angels are on your side.*[6]

As when he had visited southern Africa many years before, Roland usually made a point of addressing his arguments to European Christians:

> *. . . in this country I have felt (rightly or wrongly) that the Native peoples would resent the application to them of*

---

[5]*Times of East Africa*, 28 May 1932.
[6]Sermon note for 29.ix.1935: Rhodes House collection.

*anything which was rejected by the white people for them-
selves, and that consequently the example might perhaps be
better set by the white Christians first if possible.*[7]

Nevertheless, he found no difficulty in communicating
with Africans: *Among the Mashona in Southern Rhodesia,* he
recalled, *I set out the Apostolic practice as closely as I could . . . I asked
him why he thought I spoke like that. To my surprise he answered:
'Because you understand our customs'. The Apostolic system is so
simple, that it can be apprehended by men in every stage of education,
and civilization . . .*[8]

One of his nephews remembers 'Uncle Roland' telling him
of a conversation he had had with an indigenous Kenyan chief,
more or less along these lines:

Chief: *Other missionaries say that I should discard two of
my three wives because polygamy is illegal.* *

Roland: *I say so, too. It is illegal in England, and I am
English. But this is Africa. You are the Chief—the
Judge. Don't ask me I am a visitor who has brought
you Good News: God loves you, and your wives,
and your tribesmen; and He wants you all to love
one another. And I have introduced you to the Holy
Spirit, and told you that He would explain how to
behave. You have a very difficult problem about
love. So ask Him.*

Chief: *I have asked Him, and the Spirit says I won't be
loving them if I cast them out to starve, or to become
prostitutes. So I shan't. But the other missionaries
are angry.*

Roland: *So ought I to be. But you are the Chief, aren't you?
Just stand up for yourself. I'll back you up. I'm your
friend.*

---

[7]Letter written from Durban to the Bishop of Johannesburg (25.9.1926).

[8]See R. Allen & A. McLeish, *Devolution & its Real Significance* (World
Dominion Press, 1927), p. 11.

Unconventional approaches like this are reflected in many of Roland's frequent letters to the local press, in which he crossed swords over such issues with leaders of the Kenyan Church establishment, such as Archdeacon Owen of Kavirondo. Eventually the Bishop forbade Roland to preach in Anglican churches—although he was still permitted to celebrate Communion, and to conduct such ceremonies as weddings and baptisms for the many families who admired him.

Before the Bishop's interdict, Roland had had the opportunity to help out several clergy, by taking care of their parishes while they were away sick, or on holiday. In 1932 he was at Kiminini on Mount Elgon, and in 1936 he did service at Nakuru. In particular he spent most of 1934 in Rumuruti parish in northern Kenya as *locum* whilst the clergyman in charge was on furlough. He and Beatrice looked back on this as one of their happiest periods in Kenya. While they were in Rumuruti, in fear of what might happen if Roland were to fall ill, Grannie learned to drive a car, even though by now she had reached an age of more than three-score-years-and-ten.

Roland's fine head of snow white hair used to impress deeply the Kenya Africans, who share all their continent's great respect for elders. On several occasions embarrassment was caused, because most of the Africans present took it for granted that the *Bwana Mzee* (the old gentleman) must be the important visitor, since he was so conspicuously senior in years to such personages as the Colonial Governor, the Provincial Commissioner, or the Bishop.

Later in the 1930s Granfer often took services, especially at St. Mark's Church in Nairobi's Parklands suburb. But after a while he began to express exasperation that the church members kept expecting him to 'fill gaps', instead of persuading the Bishop to appoint the 'voluntary clergy' that he advocated. So, exactly thirty-two years after his circular letter 'To the Parishioners of Chalfont St. Peter', on 26th November 1939 Roland felt obliged to send out another letter of resignation, this time 'To the Communicants at St. Mark's Church' (see Appendix 6). In this he refused to continue this 'filling of gaps': *I would gladly serve at St. Mark's if my service helped you out of the mire,* he wrote, *but I cannot serve, if my service helps you to remain in it.*

Once again in his life, standing on principle brought Roland to resign his professional ministry, and left him in a quandary:

> *I could no longer assist the stipendiary system. But then could I, as a priest, accept the ministration of stipendiary clergy? . . . When I declined to assist, could I accept? I thought that hardly decent. So I took to celebrating at home with B . . . I was in a cleft stick.*[9]

As the Second World War continued, and many of Kenya's Anglican clergy were unavoidably called away, Roland must to some extent have relented, because between 1941 and 1945, I can myself recall frequently going to church with him and Grannie, when he was conducting services (without sermon!) at St. Mark's, or celebrating the Eucharist in the Cathedral. Moreover, his pugnacious temperament seems to have mellowed a little. In a letter to his son he displays a more relaxed attitude than heretofore: *I should be certain that wiping out the abomination of the professional stipendiary clergy system with one sweep would do much more harm than good. The step must come slowly & by degrees.*

Writing to her father in mid-1942, Priscilla remarks that: *I was much struck with your saying how you seem able now to make more sense of other people's points of view & to understand how they have it.*

A few years after settling in Kenya, at the request of the World Dominion Press, Roland composed a rather idiosyncratic biography of his old friend and benefactor, called: *S.J.W. Clark: a Vision of Missions.* As Roland frankly admits, it is not a 'life', but rather a study of Clark's thought: and although Roland was well aware that *it is impossible to do what I have tried to do without some of that interpretation which is the danger of translation,* it is unquestionable that the book expresses at least as much of Roland's own thought as that of Clark's, because it

---

[9]See *Reform of the Ministry, op. cit.,* p. 198.

was not written to magnify Clark, in an effort to recover for him a name and place: it is written in the hope of encouraging those who have seen his vision, recalling it to their minds, and perhaps increasing their number.[10]

This book was published in 1937. Otherwise, although he continued to write in a desultory way after settling in East Africa—*My husband was writing up to the end,* Grannie told Sir Kenneth Grubb—it was apparently without much thought of publication (apart from his frequent letters to the local press, and the occasional longer article submitted—but seldom published—to several of the learned and religious journals in England).

One incipient study, which he was working in his last years to improve was a 'Socratic dialogue' between two devils—a satirical study largely completed by 1930, before he left Beaconsfield. The concept was not unlike that of the best-seller by C.S. Lewis, *The Screwtape Letters*—a book which Roland very much enjoyed. In fact the appearance of *Screwtape* in 1942 may well have deterred Granfer from pursuing further the possible publication of *Satan & Beelzebub*, since his work might so easily have been thought to be no more than plagiarism. This dialogue, reproduced at Appendix 5, vividly demonstrates how exasperating Granfer's work could be for conventional missionaries, unable to conceive of their work in any but an institutionalized form.

Another book also reached quite an advanced stage —'*Voces populi de parabolis Christi*':
I sat down to write what men in the crowd who heard the Parables of Christ said about them, explains Roland in his preface. *They criticized him, they contradicted him, without any feeling of irreverence. The idea that the parables were the words of God and therefore not subject to any criticism . . . never entered the head of any of them . . . I think my readers will recognize many of those ideas as familiar, and I*

---

[10]*op. cit.,* p. 167.

159

hope that, seeing them set down without comment, men who often let them pass thoughtlessly will weigh them again and accept or reject them with conviction. Sketches looking at over two dozen parables in this way exist in draft form. In *Reform of the Ministry*, published more than twenty years after his death, Roland's draft preface may be found, together with eight expressions of different opinions by 'bystanders' who are discussing just one of the parables—*The Good Samaritan.*

A third work-in-progress in those last years brings together much of his later thought. This is a study entitled by Roland *The Ministry of Expansion: the Priesthood of the Laity*—a carefully reasoned refutation of the *teaching which strangles us . . . commonly found in the writings of two great theologians, Bishop Gore and Dr. Moberly:*

> *Their theory of the Apostolic Succession,* claims Roland, *appears to me legal, formal, strained, and based upon extremely doubtful interpretations both of the language of the New Testament and of the passages from the early Church Fathers which they quote. They fail to convince me even within their limits.*

> *I am a priest,* he continues emphatically, *and I know that grace is given in ordination for the work of the ministry; but . . . I would rather be a Quaker than admit that Sacramental grace was given to me to hinder others from grace.*

The draft pamphlet appears complete and is, I believe, of lively contemporary interest. But of that much more learned scholars must be the judges, if ever it be published.[11]

---

[11]The draft manuscripts/typescripts of all these documents are on deposit in Oxford at Rhodes House with Roland's other papers.

CHAPTER XIV

Faithful Soldier and Servant

**'a little wooden house on concrete stilts,
with a corrugated iron roof'**

Although, as we have seen, Roland continued his theological polemics in a desultory manner, he had found something completely new to interest him in Kenya. Probably few men in their mid-sixties would contemplate trying to acquire a completely new language; but Roland settled down to learning Swahili. He never spoke it well, but he rapidly learned to read the very difficult literary Swahili of the East African coast, and began to make English translations of some of the epic poetry and historical writings of the 19th and early 20th centuries. His son had swiftly become a notable Swahili scholar and also a collector of manuscripts. Iohn rendered some of these manuscripts from the Arabic script into Roman, and helped his father with complexities of language: but the bulk of the translation work was Roland's own.

Five of Granfer's translations were published, although only three of them during his lifetime. As early as 1936/37 the first of these, 'The Story of Mbega,' appeared in the first three numbers of Tanganyika Notes & Records, a learned journal still being published, of which Iohn was a founder editor. The last was not printed until 1961. As can be seen from an article as early as 1920, Roland had long been sensitive to Islamic thought and doctrine;[1] In 1928 he stayed with Dr. Mohamed Hasan of the University of Dacca, who had visited Amenbury, and with whom he evidently had long discussions. However, this work on Swahili materials, together with his son's contemporary experiences, first in the Sudan and now on the coast of Tanganyika, made him even more aware of the worth of other

---

[1]'Islam and Christianity in the Sudan', *International Review of Mission*, IX/36 (October 1920), pp. 531-543. In Roland's copy of an article by the Bishop of Madras (*The East & the West*, 18/72 (October 1920)) there may be found the following revealing manuscript note:

'What is the difference between Moslem elementary education and Xtn elementary education.

1. Moslem is religious: the pupil goes to learn religion & incidentally other things, & incidentally is enough - 'all these things are added'

   Xtn missionary schools teach other things & incidentally religion.

2. The knowledge of the Koran, or even capacity to read it, is a prize & a mark of distinction.

   Children in Xtn schs are taught to read & then have nothing to read if they have only a Bible to read. Power to read the Bible is valueless. Nobody wants that, unless he wants the pay of a teacher.

3. Moslem relig. elem. ed. finds its end in itself.

   Xtn relig. elem. ed. must justify itself by attainment of a secular end.

4. Moslem ed. is relig.

   Xtn ed. is'   [*end of note !*]

cultures' symbolism, and the danger of brushing it aside contemptuously in the name of a westernized Christianity.

When posted to the piously Islamic coastal area of Tanganyika, Iohn's early experiences in the Sudan prompted him to seek out learned Muslims and to enter into debate with them. The wisdom and integrity of these scholars—first and foremost the learned *Qadhi* (civil judge) of Tanga, Sheikh Ali Hemedi el Buhriy—made a deep and lasting impression:

> *It is all very disturbing to a Christian . . . Muslims seem to practise their beliefs more thoroughly than Christians. It often seems that to find the Christian virtues it is necessary to go to the Muslims, and the reason is that the Muslim has never succeeded in dividing his life into two watertight compartments, secular and religious . . .*

> *Muslims and Christians,* he concludes, in a talk given in the 1960s, *hate each other more cordially than most groups of the human race . . . This is the hate of near neighbours, who are so close to each other that they fear that any concession may breach the wall between them and let in the enemy. I have tried all my life to breach that wall and let in a friend . . . I could not accept that people were totally wrong who believed a very great deal of what I believe myself and who often act on their beliefs better than I do myself. Nor could I treat them as enemies, when they were engaged on the same search for truth as myself . . . Surely in this century, when the devil of materialism is so powerful, those who do believe in God should make a truce. Let us fight the devil first, and when we have defeated him, let us return to our own quarrel—if it still seems worth while.*[2]

In 1938 Iohn transferred from the Education Department to Tanganyika's provincial administration. Prevented by indifferent eyesight from joining the armed forces, by 1940 he had become a District Commissioner in the remote Southern Province,

---

[2]'Muslims in East Africa', *African Ecclesiastical Review* (July 1965).

far away from any schools for English-speaking children. In consequence from the age of eight, during the war years 1940 to 1945, I was myself sent to a primary boarding school near Nairobi. Kenton College had (and still has) premises quite close to the location of my grandparents' home: but its buildings were requisitioned for use as a military hospital during the war. So throughout my five years' attendance at the school, it was transferred to the former Westwood Park Hotel on the slopes of the Ngong Hills, some ten miles west of Nairobi city.

Grannie and Granfer had by that time settled down in what was then called the Hurlingham Road—now Argwings-Kodhek Road—in a little wooden house on concrete stilts, with a corrugated iron roof and an outside privy, and an extensive, if rather unkempt, garden full of pepper-trees and frangipani, cannas and zinnias and plumbago, all surrounded by a formidable hedge of thorny sisal plants. That neighbourhood was still very much on the fringes of Nairobi: I can myself recall seeing gnus and gazelles in the swampy valley at the bottom of the garden. And in a letter to Priscilla in April 1939, Granfer reports: *Last night a great beast came up just behind the boys' house: your mother and I both heard that deep voice. I thought that the animal was just outside our window and I asked her what she thought it was. This morning I asked the boys, and they said 'Simba tu' ('Only a lion').*

So I spent most half-term leaves and public holidays with my grandparents; and sometimes longer vacations also, not only in 1942, when my parents went to spend Iohn's home leave in South Africa, but also whenever it was inexpedient for me to try to make the difficult journey to my father's current district— often more than 1,000 miles distant, over extremely rugged terrain.

It was a quiet and orderly household, very firmly ruled by Grannie. Every morning she would unlock the larder with the bunch of keys chained to her girdle, and dole out to the cook and to the houseboy the requisite provisions—foodstuffs, polish, disinfectant, etc—needed for that day. She was a real martinet, a stickler for good behaviour and impeccable table manners. I well remember, for example, being scolded for 'tinkling' my teaspoon against the side of my cup when stirring, and—worse still, it seemed—for stirring widdershins instead of clockwise.

She was extremely protective of Granfer, who was at that time often in poor health, when not seriously ill, and otherwise deeply engrossed in his Swahili translations and other writing. She was particularly quick to tell us children that we must not tire him; so I practically never had any opportunity for long conversations with him. However, it was during one of those holidays that I remember asking him whether I could read his books, and receiving the reply: *Oh yes, you can read them by all means—but you won't understand them.* When I looked a little crestfallen, he went on to explain: *I don't think anyone is going to understand them until I've been dead ten years . . .*

I had not been particularly surprised by Granfer's first remark. It has sometimes been said of him that he could not suffer fools gladly. But that view is mistaken. He could in fact be endlessly patient with genuinely stupid people. On the other hand, the intellectual shortcomings of people whom he believed to be intelligent tended to exasperate him. His sister-in-law (Willoughby's wife, Iohn's and Priscilla's much loved Aunt Nellie) once complained *His talk made me feel so stupid!* And a friend of Kenya days remarks that Roland

> *was adept at giving the opposite viewpoint to a speaker, merely to get things going! He had a wonderful sense of humour, but could be difficult too! He . . . was a very human person, conscious of his own frailties, but more aware than many of us of his own powers of intellect, which perhaps at times made him very impatient of fools: and so thus he could be very difficult with 'lesser' mortals.*

One of those lesser mortals, a nurse engaged to take care of Roland when he was convalescent, *had not a good word to say for Roland's temper!*[3]

---

[3]Mrs. Barbara Saben, CBE - personal communication.

Roland was acutely aware of such shortcomings in his character. When he met an expert anthropologist in Assam, of whom he noted in his diary that *like men who know much more of some subject than anyone they meet, he is apt to be assertive,* he went on ruefully: *So am I.* Again, he comments: *it is a most obnoxious thing to enunciate as divine truth a statement which the other man does not recognise as divine truth, and then say or imply 'You're damned if you do not follow/obey me'. I fear that is what the Bishop feels that I have been doing. I suspect that I have been lacking in courtesy.*

As a chess player my ineptitude bored Granfer, so we seldom tried to play that game together. And he quickly demonstrated to me the futility of noughts-and-crosses between intelligent players. The only game that he really enjoyed playing with me was Battleships, because it gave scope for logical skill as well as luck. But he much enjoyed observing other people playing games, and would sit attentively listening as my friends or my sisters and I argued over tactics, and would readily act as referee if the occasion arose.

My grandparents had a small saloon car—a Hillman, I think. They bought this in 1939 to replace a Ford. Roland at that time told Priscilla that: *it is delightful to drive; but it is not quite like a Ford in that bumps do shake its anatomy. Little things, but, after the journey to Mombasa, stays, &c, were shaken, and an axle bent.*

Granfer would sometimes take us for a drive to visit family friends or to have a peaceful picnic in one of the city's parks or on the Ngong Hills. At one such picnic—a children's birthday party in Nairobi's Arboretum—I recall that Grannie compressed history for me in a rather startling manner, by reminiscing about a picnic which she herself had attended long ago in a London park: that occasion had been arranged by two old ladies in memory of yet a *third* picnic, which they had attended at Versailles in the garden of *Le Petit Trianon* when they were children—and their hostess had been Queen Marie Antoinette!

Roland hated jingoistic nationalism, and did not endear himself to Kenya's fiercely patriotic British settlers by, for example, remarking that the Church should not *wrap up the Bible inside the Union Jack, lest both be thrown out together.* During the early years of the Second World War, Roland found himself drawn into speaking up, and writing to the press, against anti-German hostility among the settlers, much of which was un-thinkingly directed against the unfortunate Jewish refugees from Hitler, of whom there were considerable numbers in East Africa. He pointed out the folly of one correspondent's alleged hatred for all things German: *I might ask him whether he 'hates' all drugs invented by German chemists . . . whether he 'hates' all German music . . . 'blind hatred' is not Christian, not even human . . .* But his admonitions often fell on deaf ears: *Mr. Allen may claim the Hun, Wop, or Yellow Dog as a brother, I do not,* fumed one of the settlers in a letter to the same local paper.[4]

Roland frequently visited the internment camp at Kabete, where Germans, Hungarians, and other 'enemy aliens' were being held; he would sometimes read Shakespeare with some of the inmates, and he would take up issues for them with the British authorities. One of the Jews in the camp, a Mr. Hermann Fliess, who was a widower from Hamburg, had had experience in East Africa since 1909. He had been appointed camp leader, to represent all its inmates, even the Nazis.

One day Roland and Beatrice learned that Mr. Fliess had a motherless son and daughter in Nairobi. The Allens went to pay a call on these two children and were horrified to find both of them running wild, wholly neglected by a feckless landlady. They removed them at once: the son, Ralph, was placed with a neighbour—an eminent architect; and the 12-year-old daugh-ter, Valerie, came to live in the Allens' own home for nearly four years, until—with Grannie in her eighties and Granfer's health deteriorating—places were found for both children at local boarding schools. During those years Valerie attended the near-by Kenya High School for Girls as a day-boarder, and was sent for her holidays to various farms, where there were settlers who

---

[4]See *East African Standard*, 14 and 24 June 1941 and 15 January 1943.

were rather more charitable than Roland's antagonists in his newspaper correspondence.

Valerie remembers Roland as *a fine-looking man who was both kind and also rather stern and austere*. She recounts:

> *I very much wished to become a Christian at that time, and was hurt when Roland told my father that I only wanted to be confirmed in a white frock, like my friends, and that I should not be allowed to do so until I was older. Of course I know now he was quite right, but there was more to it than the frock—I was deeply impressed by the Church of England service.*[5]

Apart from his Swahili translations, Granfer's chief relaxation in his declining years was the solving of chess problems. These used to be sent out to him from England by Priscilla and by one of his nephews; and he used to exchange them with his principal chess partner in Nairobi, a Dr. Goldstein, who was another of the Jewish refugees from Nazi Germany. Dr.Goldstein, like other anti-Nazi internees with useful professional skills, had early been released from detention to work as a medical doctor in Nairobi. (Valerie's father, likewise, had gone off to Somalia to do useful work in Mogadishu).

I remember once asking Dr. Goldstein which of them was the better player, to which he replied: *Your grandfather, of course*. He went on to recount a story about one of Granfer's long sea voyages in the 1920s. Apparently Roland had been the only person on board the ship that could give one of his fellow passengers a decent game. *Mark you, I hardly ever beat him*, Granfer was quick to interpose, *and only when he was tired—or experimenting, perhaps*. But that was not surprising, for his opponent had been none other than the longtime world champion, the great José Capablanca himself!

Soon after the end of the war, in September 1945, my parents set out with me and my two sisters on our way home to England. Father had obtained permission for us to travel through Uganda

---

[5]Personal communication.

and the Sudan down the Nile to Cairo, where Priscilla was then serving as a WAAF officer at British headquarters. On our last morning in Nairobi, in the knowledge that we were most unlikely ever all to meet again, Granfer administered Communion in both kinds to the whole family, including Grannie and us three grandchildren, although at seven, nine and thirteen years old none of us were yet confirmed.

Iohn had sent off a letter to the Sudan to his Muslim acquaintance of 20 years earlier; but he received no reply. Very early one morning, however, as our train drew into a little station some distance south of Khartoum, my two sisters and I were brusquely plucked from our bunks and tumbled hastily into our clothes. The old scholar had died a year or two previously; but there on the station platform were his seven surviving sons, two of them now government ministers of cabinet rank, all cheerfully giving up their sleep in order to welcome their late father's Christian friend!

That Communion service was the last time that any of us three grandchildren saw Granfer alive. After Iohn's home leave Winkie stayed in England, to settle us into schools there, whilst Iohn travelled out alone for his next tour of duty in Tanganyika.

Meanwhile Roland was still busy thinking and writing. His last published thoughts seem to be the closing letter of a correspondence about evolution and the existence of God: . . . *it is inconceivable that Chaos can out of itself evolve Cosmos. All religious men say that 'God' is the inevitable assumption.*[6]

But he was a very sick man now, and on June 9th, 1947, he died: *His mind remained clear and alert until the morning before his death, and he died without pain.*[7]

As one admirer has written:

His translation of Utenzi wa kutawafu nabii—'The Release of the Prophet'—*sympathetically and sensitively conveys the author's deep understanding of how the Prophet*

---

[6]*East African Standard,* 4th February 1947.
[7]Priscailla Allen, *op. cit.,* p. 11.

Muhammad met the Angel Azrael, Allah's messenger of death. Those who were with Roland Allen at the end say that he too was on friendly and fearless terms with Azrael as he prepared for a quiet move from one life to another.[8]

The burial service was conducted by the Bishop of Mombasa. His grave in Nairobi's City Park is marked by a simple stone cross.[9]

Although Beatrice was over five years older than her husband, she survived Roland by more than a dozen years. Apart from visits of a few weeks to see Iohn and Winkie in Arabia, where her son had become the Deputy British Agent for the Western Aden Protectorate,[10] and later in Mwanza, when he had returned to Tanganyika for his last years as a colonial officer, she continued to live in Nairobi, in the little wooden house.

Then in 1958, for the last two years of her life, she went with Priscilla to be near her and Iohn in Kampala, where both of her children had coincidentally accepted appointments in the University of East Africa at Makerere. She died there in January 1960, in her ninety-seventh year: her grave in the Jinja Road cemetery is still identifiable,[11] although sadly mutilated during Uganda's recent violent history, when most of the European gravestones were allegedly used for target practice by Idi Amin's troops.

---

[8]Noel Q. King, 'Last Years in East Africa', *Reform of the Ministry, op. cit.*, p. 176.

[9]The inscription on the pedestal reads: ROLAND ALLEN, Clerk in Holy Orders, 1868-1947, I AM THE RESURRECTION AND THE LIFE SAITH THE LORD.

[10]Later to become independent as South Yemen.

[11]The name has gone, but the grave can be identified by the inscription placed on it by her children — the same words as later to be inscribed on Iohn's and Winkie's own: *I go to a Glorious Resurrection.*

Epilogue

As we remarked in the prologue to this memoir, nowadays few of Roland Allen's ideas seem particularly startling: most of them have, indeed, become accepted as 'main stream', and it is difficult to realise that he was for so long looked upon as an isolated and irrelevant eccentric.

The full handover of missionary churches to indigenous Christians is in almost all parts of the world accepted practice. Even in England's established Church, clergy have become much more reluctant to dispense such sacraments as baptism and marriage as if they were no more than social niceties. Far and wide the Eucharist has become the normal Sunday service, central to the life of the Church. The charismatic movement has emphasized the Holy Spirit's role as the dynamic for Christian mission. The importance of the mission of the laity is ever more widely recognized. The ordination of non-stipendiary Anglican priests is a familiar, if still reluctant, move towards Roland's conception of voluntary clergy. And pressures for ecumenical cohesion are commonplace—though not yet sufficiently, perhaps, as Lesslie Newbigin points out,[1] between all the innumerable small independent movements which have in recent years tended to be at the cutting edge of Christian outreach.

What is more, although *He was trained an Anglican, went to China as an Anglican, and died an Anglican,*[2] missiologists and theologians over a very wide spectrum of churchmanship have come to recognise the relevance of Roland's teaching regarding their own concerns. As he remarks, for example: *I use about the*

---

[1] See *Foreword*, p. xv above.
[2] Brammer, *op. cit.*, p. 177.

orders of the ministry the terms natural to one who believes in apostolic succession. But the general force of my argument would not be affected if I used the terms natural to a Presbyterian or a Wesleyan.[3]

He was a New Testament man, points out one scholar: *In all of his major writings there are only two brief references to the Old Testament.*[4] Some evangelicals have thought his theology too preoccupied with the sacramental, some liberals have thought him too close to fundamentalism, some high churchmen have thought him suspiciously anti-clerical: but all of these have been provoked by his teaching to re-think their own ideas. *This is the way of Christ and His Apostles,* says Roland, over and over and over again, whatever the point at issue: all his critics have been—and are—obliged to confront that assertion.

Even in his old age the prophet did not rest. In 1943 he was still writing to Iohn: *In the Church there is a point at which rebellion is justifiable for the good of the Church, not for any personal end.* Are any of his ideas still having any impact? Can anything still be learnt, either from the ones for which his name has become familiar, or from those which he began to articulate only in his waning years? Is it really true that even today, in Lesslie Newbigin's words, the reader of Roland Allen's writings is likely to *find before long that many of his accustomed ideas are being questioned by a voice more searching than the word of man*? [5]

There exist multifarious evidences of his influence, direct or indirect, over several decades, on churches and missionaries in many lands and of many sects. Numerous allusions may be found in the books and articles cited as references in this memoir. It would be very far beyond the knowledge and capacity of the present writer, or the scope of this book, to attempt to follow up and identify all of these, ranging as they do from the rapid growth of the indigenous church in China after 1976, and the East African Revival, to changing concepts of the priesthood

---

[3] *Missionary Methods, op. cit.,* p. 9.

[4] Brammer, *op. cit.,* p.179.

[5] Foreword to American edition of *Missionary Methods–St.Paul's or Ours?*

in Ecuador and other parts of Latin America, and among the Canadian Inuit peoples.

What seems remarkable, however, is how many of today's debates are foreshadowed somewhere or other in Roland's writings. True, it does not appear that he ever addressed himself to the possibility of ordaining women to the Anglican priesthood: in discussions of 1 Timothy 3:2-7 and Titus 1:6-9 he takes for granted the "husband of one wife", and so forth. But it seems very doubtful that he would have found these Pauline phrases supreme to his concept of the "priesthood which belongs inherently to all Christians". And he had a great admiration for women's perceptiveness. Time and again in his diary during his travels in India, for example, he remarks how frequently the women he spoke to were among the first to comprehend and to approve his theological arguments.

The only faintly relevant evidence I can myself supply is the fact that I observed him to respond with no more than a melancholy smile when somebody (I think it was my mother) cited Dr. Johnson's notorious remark that *a woman's preaching is like a dog's walking on his hinder legs. It is not done well; but you are surprised to find it done at all.*[6] At the time I attributed Granfer's lack of enthusiasm to the fact that he was unwell. But now I am not so sure.

It is perhaps suggestive that it was the Chinese branch of the Anglican Church, in which Roland commenced his ministry, which was the first to alter its canons to provide for the voluntary clergy he advocated; and it was that same Chinese Church which was to be the first to ordain an Anglican woman priest.

Another indicator seems to lie, paradoxically, in Roland's refusal to condemn polygamy among Africans and native North

---

[6] Boswell's *Life of Johnson*, 31 July 1763.

[7] See especially Chapter V of *'Sponx'*. Bishop Azariah told Roland that his elder sister, Mercy, had read this; and remarked that *to his surprise she was not shocked at the chapter on morals which offended him.* See *Reform of the Ministry, op. cit.,* p. 107.

Americans.[7] This demonstrates that, whilst he was insistent on advocating the *methods* of St. Paul, he was in no way insisting that the accidents of Pauline *society* should dictate perpetually to those living in another culture. (St. Paul, for example, did not condemn the practice of slavery). Others have noted how Roland's admiration for women emerged even in the hobby of his old age, when he was translating Swahili poetry.[8]

Furthermore, even if Roland might have entertained doubts about women's ordination, what was of surpassing importance in his eyes was the regular and frequent administration of the sacraments. As he remarks to his son in 1943:

> *I believe in Sacraments, and therefore believe that they are incapable of being destroyed by any such error, but that on the contrary local errors are, and must be, simply steps towards their glorification.*

> What is more, *I cannot help noticing that some people most exalt the divine order of priesthood just when that order is proving itself to the majority of men most in need of reform. It is then that Schism is made the deadliest of sins.*

There is no comfort in these writings for opponents of women's ordination.

Be that as it may, several other of the ideas he propounded towards the end of his life are even now, half a century later, still so unorthodox that some of them are as yet only beginning to become subjects of controversy.

To provide the sacraments, Roland pointed out, it is not at all necessary to have the expensive paraphernalia of a consecrated church building. They could—and should, he came to believe—be administered by the head of any and every Christian household within his own home: although always within a framework of order and unity, as he insists in his advice to his son (see Appendix 3 below). In a tentative fashion Roland began in his final years to raise this question of the 'house church', and

---

[8] See King, *op, cit.*, pp. 173 and 175ff.

to propound even more radical theories. To take just a few of these: [9]

> Roland had found one authority, the Church, *which practised, and by its practice taught, what was false by its own theory;* then what about another authority—the Bible itself? Roland's own most influential books—e.g. *Missionary Methods* and *Pentecost & the World*—are rooted and grounded in scripture to such an extent that he has been called a fundamentalist. But now: *Let a man once cease to pass over difficult passages, and then what happens? Serious consequences follow . . . to accept as equally divinely inspired the book Ecclesiastes and the Sermon on the Mount was absurd . . .*

> Again: *The Gospels are not law books. Christians in establishing Christian Law, standards, codes, have gone back from Christ to Moses . . . pure principle has been too high for most of us.*

> Moreover: *It seems to me that by admitting the validity of lay Baptism* [a doctrine accepted even by the Roman Catholic church, as was evidenced by the instructions given to Civil Defence workers during the Second World War] *any necessary and essential relation between Orders and the administration of sacraments is denied, and any argument for the essential necessity of Orders for the valid administration of Holy Communion is rendered absurd.* So much for 'the Tractarian tradition'!

> Until at last: *Slowly I began to think of the Church of England, perhaps even 'Christianity' as known to us, as something temporary, a stage in the history of religion, and local. It was plainly incapable of any universality . . . Roman*

---

[9] All the following quotations are taken from a manuscript notebook written in 1943 and 1944, and reproduced under the title 'The Family Rite' in *Reform of the Ministry, op.cit.*, pp. 191-219.

*Catholicism made great claims to solve the difficulty by
infallible utterances, but I soon saw that it was simply a
form of ecclesiastical Nazism, and
could no more endure than political Nazism could endure . . .*

The loneliness and seeming arrogance of his position was
uncomfortable and worrying for Roland. Much like Isaiah, he
felt he was no more than a man of unclean lips, dwelling among
a people of unclean lips:

*Was I, who knew that other men, much wiser and more
learned than myself, had gone far astray, to set myself up as
sole authority for myself? Alter, even a little, some element
in my birth and up-bringing, and I might be taking a very
different view. To decide great religious issues for myself was
plainly a very dangerous and slippery business . . . But
where I was really touched,* he concludes, *I was convinced
by my own inside. I was simply compelled to do that. I had
no choice.*

Many, if not most of these ideas of Roland's 'declining
years' may seem to us as eccentric and impracticable as his
earlier ones seemed to his own contemporaries. Some of them
appear to be verging on heresy—an annoyance and a scandal for
the Church and its establishment.

Perhaps. But possibly some of Roland Allen's prophetic
insights have, even today, still to be seen for what they are. Let
us leave the last word with a Roman Catholic—a Jesuit—who
had been introduced to Roland's writings by a Lutheran colleague:

*I do not think he would have expected us, or wanted us, to
come to the identical conclusions on every point that he
himself reached over sixty years ago . . . But the main and
general insights and questions of this remarkable man are as
valid today as they were when they first stunned and
disturbed the Church of his day.*[10]

---

[10] Vincent J. Donovan sj, *Christianity Rediscovered* (S.C.M. Press, 1978), p. 32f.

APPENDIX 1

Some relationships mentioned in the text

The Allen family

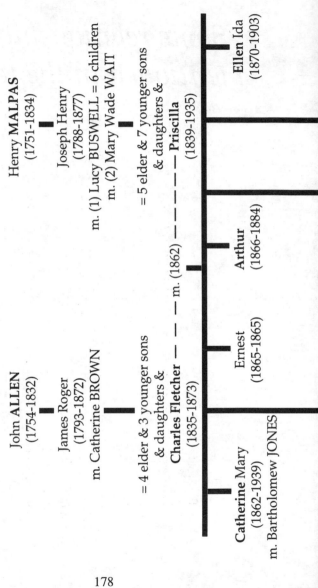

Henry MALPAS
(1751-1834)

Joseph Henry
(1788-1877)

m. (1) Lucy BUSWELL = 6 children
m. (2) Mary Wade WAIT

= 5 elder & 7 younger sons
& daughters &
Priscilla
(1839-1935)

John ALLEN
(1754-1832)

James Roger
(1793-1872)

m. Catherine BROWN

= 4 elder & 3 younger sons
& daughters &
Charles Fletcher
(1835-1873)

— — — m. (1862) — — —

Catherine Mary
(1862-1939)
m. Bartholomew JONES

Ernest
(1865-1865)

Arthur
(1866-1884)

Ellen Ida
(1870-1903)

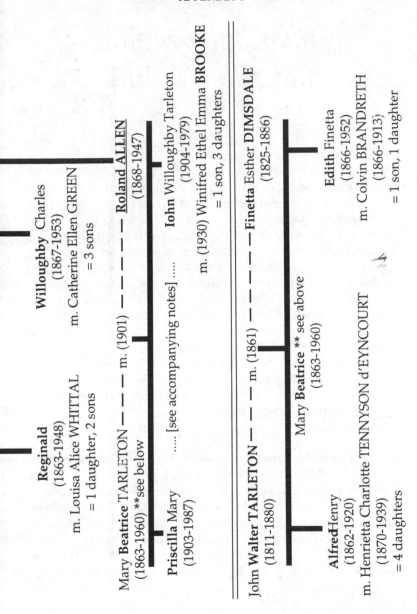

Summary biographies of Roland Allen's children

Priscilla Mary Allen *(1903-1987)* read *litterae humaniores* (classical 'mods & greats') at St. Hugh's College, Oxford. Subsequently she spent most of her life as a librarian in East Africa, first of all at the Macmillan Memorial Library in Nairobi, and then (after her war service in England and Egypt with the WAAF) at the Medical Research Laboratory in the same city. In 1958 she moved to Uganda to establish the medical section of the Makerere University library at Mulago teaching hospital; and from 1965 to 1968 she was librarian for the University of Addis Ababa in Ethiopia. On retirement at age 65, she returned to Nairobi, where for a few years more she became the first professional librarian for Kenya's National Museum.

During the 1939-1945 war she resumed her childhood hobby of bird-watching; in later years she became a renowned ornithologist and a very knowledgeable botanist, whose meticulous notes are still treasured by the East African Natural History Society—of which she was a founder member, long-time secretary, and in due course president.

Iohn Willoughby Tarleton Allen *(1904-1979)* also read 'mods & greats' at St. John's College, Oxford; and then, after two years with the Sudan Plantations Syndicate in the Gezira Scheme, went to Tanganyika (as it then was), firstly as an education officer, and from 1937 in the Provincial Administration. In 1930 he married Winifred Ethel Emma Brooke—'Winkie'. Transferred in 1947 to become Deputy British Agent in the Western Aden Protectorate (nowadays south Yemen), he returned to Tanganyika in 1953.

Leaving the Colonial Service in 1958, he moved to Makerere University College in Uganda, as both secretary of the East African Swahili Committee, and warden of a new student hall of residence. Thence, with funds from the Rockefeller Foundation and other sources, he and his wife Winkie travelled up and down the East African coast and its islands, undertaking research and the collection of Swahili documents and tape-recordings. From 1968 to 1970 he became Director of the University of Dar-es-Salaam's Institute of Swahili Research. And finally he and Winkie were recruited by the government of Denmark to spend three years devising and teaching specialist Swahili language programmes for Danish aid volunteers at Tengeru near Arusha.

An interest in Swahili, especially in early poetry and writings in Arabic script, which he began to collect during his first years on East Africa's coast, developed into an almost unsurpassed expertise regarding the language and the Sha'afi Islamic culture and law of the Swahili people; although an active Christian, he was revered as a sufi—a seeker after truth. Many leading African poets and scholars were close personal friends, and he was the advisor and editor for Tanzania's national poet, Sha'aban Robert. After his final retirement—even on his deathbed—he continued to study Swahili manuscripts, many of which he edited meticulously during his long career.

Iohn and Winkie had one son and three daughters. One daughter died in childhood, but the other three children flourished, and in due course married and raised eleven of their own children, although all of these were born long after their great-grandfather Roland's death.

The resignation letter

To the Parishioners of
Chalfont St. Peter

Chalfont St. Peter.
November 25th, 1907.

MY FRIENDS,

I am very anxious that you should all understand the reason why I am resigning my work here.

From the earliest times the Church has always asserted her right to ordain the conditions on which she admits people to her privileges and to reject those who deliberately and persistently break her laws, which are the laws of God. This principle is definitely asserted in several places (see the Rubrics before the Holy Communion and the Burial Offices) and tacitly implied everywhere in our own Prayer Book. But in process of time it has come to pass in England that on the one hand nearly everybody in the country is, at least in name, Christian, and on the other hand the machinery by which the law of the Church was intended to be made effective has fallen into disuse, and in practice it is now almost impossible to enforce it. Thus the widest inclusion of every kind and class of man has been accompanied with a relaxation of the means by which the morality of the society was maintained. The result is that it has become customary for people who make no profession of believing the doctrines of the Church, or who make no profession of keeping the laws of the Church, to demand and use her offices as if they were theirs by natural inheritance.

In consequence we see the strange and painful sight of men and women who habitually neglect their religious duties, or who openly deny the truth of the Creeds, or who by the immorality of their lives openly defy the laws of God, standing up as Sponsors in a Christian Church, before a Christian Minister, in the presence of a Christian congregation and as representatives of the Church on behalf of a new-born child solemnly professing their desire for Holy Baptism, their determination to renounce the world, the flesh and the devil, their stedfast faith in the Creed and their willingness to obey God's holy will, whilst they know, and everyone in the Church knows, that they themselves neither do, nor intend to do, any of these things. Then they are solemnly directed to see that the child is taught the faith and practice which they set at naught. Or again, we see that sad sight of the dead body of a man who all his life denied the claim of Jesus Christ, or who set at naught the moral laws of God, brought into Christ's Church in order that a service may be read over his body which, whilst alive, he utterly scorned.

I am of course aware that no priest is legally bound to admit any but Communicants as sponsors, but immorality of life is no bar to the legal use of the Burial or Marriage Services. In the one case the law, in the other custom (more powerful often than the law) compels the acquiescence of a priest in a practice which he cannot justify.

For no one can justify these things. They undermine the fundamental principle that the Church stands for morality of life; they suggest the horrible doctrine that the Church does not regard morality as an essential part of religion. They embolden men to go on living in sin in the hope that they will not be rejected at the last. Ignorant men speak as if Christ and His Church had nothing to offer which is not the natural inheritance of every Englishman, nor any right to lay down rules and conditions on which those gifts may be obtained; because they see every man, whatever his belief or his character, admitted without question to the highest privileges which the Church can bestow.

They bring the services of the Church into disrepute and make them an open scorn. There is a horrible danger in using

Holy Services in the case of people who deny by word or deed all that is implied in them. People think and speak as if the Services of the Church were 'mere forms'. God is not mocked. Services used in the name of God are high and holy things, sources of real blessing, and to degrade them into 'mere forms' is a serious offence, of which the consequences are terribly real.

Now, as Parish Priest, it is my duty to uphold morality and to defend religion, and I feel that in acquiescing to these customs I am neither upholding morality nor defending religion. I cannot satisfy my conscience by exhorting people to refrain from doing what is wrong, and then in the last resort, if they will not listen to me, giving way to them. I have done that, I fear, too often. I have carried my exhortations to the point of seriously annoying some of you. I have entreated and advised till we both were weary, but you knew and I knew that in the end I could not absolutely refuse. In one or two cases I regret that I did not refuse; but my mind was not clear as to the right course, and I preferred to obey the law. Now I am clear: I can not and will not do these things any longer.

I am well aware of the serious character of my decision. I am not ignorant that I cannot act as I am determined to act, and yet hold any benefice in England. It has indeed been urged upon me by some that I might retain my position and wait until some serious case arose and I was forced by law to resign. I feel sure that I could, if I would, do that. I believe that so long as I acted wisely and discreetly, I should enjoy again, as I have enjoyed in the past, the sympathy and support of every communicant in this Church. But that would not be right. Legal processes are not easily understood by the poor and ignorant, and some of those who would most bitterly resent my refusal to obey the law are very poor. I will not do in the case of a poor man an action for which he cannot force me to pay the legal penalty. I think the poor man would feel a just resentment if he were treated in spiritual matters in a way which a rich man could resist by process of law. And more than that, it seems to me scarcely honest to hold and enjoy the emoluments of an office of which

I deliberately refuse to perform the legal obligations.

If that were not enough I should be compelled to resign by my sense of the very serious nature of resistance to law. I believe that passive resistance to law is sometimes a duty, but I do not believe that it is a light matter or one to be undertaken without the most serious consideration and the most deliberate determination to bear cheerfully the penalty whatever the penalty may be. A passive resistance which costs little or nothing is a passive resistance which I despise and dread. It tends to undermine an authority which the Bible tells us proceeds from God, and it is only justified by the strongest moral obligations and the most complete self-surrender to serious consequences. For me to resist the law whilst I enjoyed my office, trusting to your sympathy and support to save me from the consequences, would be, in my opinion, to commit that offence.

One form of protest, and only one, remains open to me, and that is to decline to hold an office in which I am liable to be called upon to do what I feel to be wrong. I have chosen that. I have resigned.

There remains one serious objection to all that I have said and it is an objection of which I am profoundly sensible. You are all well aware that a great many good and thoughtful men hold these positions and perform these offices without reproach, and you know that one will be found to take my place when I am gone. I am very anxious to explain this so far as I can. For the past three years I have been restrained from taking any action solely by the feeling that I must be wrong in refusing to do what so many good men can conscientiously do. I felt that I could not face the charge that I was setting myself up to be better and wiser than these men when in very truth I knew that I was not. They argue, if I understand them rightly, that they can do more good by continuing in their cures to perform these offices than by any other course. They hope to raise the standard of public opinion in these matters by continual teaching, and they can point to many signs that the standard of opinion is being so raised. They believe that it is their duty in a world of imperfection, to tolerate the imperfection which they cannot remove whilst they strive after the perfection which they desire. They think that refusal to perform these services is contrary to law, and that to resign rather than to obey is a counsel of despair which would reduce all Church work in England to chaos. They plead that acts done by the ministers of the Church are done in the name and with the authority of the whole Church, and that therefore no individual priest can be held individually responsible for acts so done. They say that the Church as a matter of history has never been free from these difficulties; that we must look forward to the quiet growth of an enlightened public opinion, and that meanwhile it is the duty of a good minister to do his best under the conditions in which he now finds himself.

These arguments are sufficient to satisfy the minds of many good men: I can only say that they do not satisfy me. I have repeatedly told you from this pulpit that I believe we ought always at all costs to act according to the dictates of our conscience — that when our conscience tells us that a thing is wrong we ought not to do it whatever the consequences may be. When a difficult question arises, when our conscience protests against some action which is commonly done by a great many good men, I think we ought carefully to enquire whether our conscience is well informed (for a conscience may be morbid or misinformed), we ought to take time and pains to make sure that we are not suffering from a delusion; but if after all that careful examination our conscience still persists in forbidding us to do it, we must obey. It is better to do anything, to suffer anything, rather than to live under the condemnation of that voice which speaks to us with the authority of God.

And I believe further that in the end it will be found that no man can better fulfil his duty to others than by strictly observing this rule. It may appear now as if obedience to conscience and the service of the Church in this place were in opposition, that to obey conscience in resigning is to abandon all hope of useful work. But I am persuaded that in the end it will be made plain that these two things which now appear to be in opposition are really one, and that I can do no service to you so true as to refuse to serve you in this. I believe that Christ's teaching about simplicity of aim, singleness of eye, is directed to just such difficulties as these; that He meant to teach us to refuse to be blinded by doctrines of expediency, by side issues; to do simply and obediently what He tells us, and that if we do that we shall find that in the end we have not missed the other. I believe that in resigning I am seeking not merely my own salvation, but your best interests and the interests of the Church of which I am a Minister.

I resign with very deep regret. I have valued most highly your sympathy, your forbearance, your ungrudging help, and as time goes on, I shall more and more feel the loss of it.

I have asked the Bishop to declare the vacancy at Christmas, and I have asked the Patrons, S. John's College in Oxford, to use all possible urgency that is agreeable with care in seeking the right man to supply my place.

Till Christmas I shall continue my work here. Then I must seek work where it may please God to call me.

Meanwhile I commend myself, the Bishop, the Patrons and the Parish to your earnest prayers. You will pray, I am sure, for me, that I may be guided aright. You will pray that it may please God to send to this parish a faithful and true Pastor.

And this may He do for His mercy's sake.

Believe me,

Your sincere friend,

ROLAND ALLEN.

Advice to an active voluntary clergyman in the Sudan

A: Note to John:[1]

November 18, 1927:
see J's diary, p.20,sq.

I can only speak as it appears to me and with diffidence.

(1) Where one is alone, as in the case cited by you, there is a sort of extension outside the external order. The Bishop cannot ordain because there is no external Church there to receive a ministry, and he can only establish a Church with a minister. The individual acts as an individual in communion with the unseen others. He is a priest for himself, not for others: for himself he needs no external credentials; but for others he does: for them he needs the authority given by the Church to him to act for the Church. Alone, his priesthood is in himself.

(2) When he is beyond the reach of the ordered life of the Church, and he acts for others and with others, he does so by mutual agreement and consent. There is no question of regularizing the ministrations within the ordered scheme of the Church, because the group is ex hypothesi beyond reach.

(3) But when he is not really beyond, but only beyond because the Bishop will not do his duty to the group and establish the Church duly, then arises a question, but, it seems

---

[1]Puzzling abbreviations have been spelled out in full in these notes.

to me, a question of the action of the Bishop, not of his. As far as he is concerned, he and his group are still beyond the Bishop.

In the light of the above, I think

(1) that we ought to teach our people that they may enjoy full Church life without episcopal sanction where they are manifestly out of reach of the Bishop, though within his nominal diocese; because our nominal dioceses are absurd, and do not represent any reality of episcopal supervision.

But this will not do instead of proper ordination, and (2) we ought to demand the proper establishment wherever two or three are united.

(3) We cannot urge men generally to exercise the priesthood of the laity for themselves alone, because its sanction is internal, and even I see that it is not easily reconciled with the social 'two or three' of Christ; and if a man is not persuaded in his own mind, he cannot act in that way.

(4) that we ought to insist that the Sacraments are really social, and that nothing can justify a man in retiring by himself alone, rather than join with his fellows, when he obviously can do so, if he wills. To do this would be schismatic. There ought to be order, and in the action of an individual for himself and on his own authority there is no apparent order. Internally there may be order, or disorder: that is a question of the spirit in which a man acts.

B: January 14, 1928 Sadiya, N.E.Assam
My dear John,

(your diary p.58?, 59, 60)

(1) You say 'I fail to see the difference between the man, who is beyond the territorial bounds of the Church through inevitable circumstances, and the man who is out of reach because the Bishop is not doing his duty'. I only distinguish from the point of view of the Bishop, not from the point of view of the man. From the point of view of the man there is no difference. And I agree with the consequent duties which you set out.

190

(2) You say 'What I feel is the necessity to encourage laymen to be ready to be moved to celebrate in either case (i.e. group? or no group?) . . . Also it is the duty of every man who wants them to have the Sacraments: but not the duty of all the members of a group to argue with their Bishop'. Here I am not sure of 'them': does 'them' = the Sacraments, or the members of the group?— i.e. A wants the group to have Sacraments, therefore *he* must argue . . .

Here I think

(a) that what is necessary is to persuade laymen that they need Christ at all, then that Sacraments are the proper form of expression and means of grace for a church (in the local sense) the members of which really do recognize Christ. I think that the isolated individual may act alone, and should be taught so, *if* he can apprehend his action in relation to the Church Universal. But the Sacraments are properly and naturally group acts. You recognize that 'much is lost by the being alone; but it seems to be giving way too much to Space-Time to consider this prohibitive'. Many men cannot escape out of the Space-Time elements; and therefore they are inhibited by isolation and the consequent tradition. Formally I think it is not prohibitive and I have said so in your case.

(b) It is when the group needs and feels the need of express church life that the church should approach the Bishop (i.e. the group of those who feel the need) and it is not sufficient for one to feel it for the others and approach the Bishop on behalf of the others, except as a mere spokesman expressing an agreed wish, and that is the same thing as if all spoke. It is not all the members individually and severally who speak and argue, but the group as a group which demands the admitted rights of a group, i.e. of a local church.

(c) At the moment it seems to me to be important to begin with the case of the small group of communicant church people, because there the case is clear and generally acknowledged; rather than to begin by arguing publicly the case of the isolated individual where the case is purely personal and the historical argument difficult, and based rather upon exceptions. Here, e.g., in Assam it is certainly the small groups of communicants with which *I* ought to begin: though if I met the man in your case I should give him the advice which I gave to you. And I certainly should not argue that the right to celebrate for himself had any basis in the 'sanctity' of the individual: I should argue not from his sanctity, but from his need and sense of need. No man is 'good enough' to celebrate under any circumstances. The grace of Christ is not a response of Christ to man's 'goodness' but to man's need and readiness to accept the grace.

Write again and tell me whether this satisfies you or not.

RA

By 'group' in every case I mean communicants, not mere nominal churchmen who do not want any sacraments at all (unless it may be baptism for their children). What I want is to persuade the 'group' that it really is 'the Church' in the place, and therefore should be established as the Church in the place with all the privileges of the Church.

P.S. I have been reading your first note (diary, p.20) again. What I said in answer was that a Bishop could only give the priesthood to *a Church* (i.e. a group of Christians who wanted to be, and could be, properly established): he could not *ordain* one man for himself alone Nor could he, I think, *ordain* under the conditions which you describe when two or three men are casually united for a brief time and then split up again. Under such circumstances I do not see how there can be *ordination*, which implies a regular and settled condition. Under such circumstances a man *may*, I think, act for himself or with the other two or three, pro tem., but then he acts either for himself, or by agreement, in which case it is mutual agreement only (as Bombay's three men at the front). Only when there is a recognisable group, which can be properly established as a church, can the Bishop officially ordain clergy for a Church (local), and I do not see how otherwise he can act. I am protesting against a priest ordained with a sort of roving commission, am I not, when I protest against itinerating clergy. There is an official cleric ordained for a local church and properly serving that church; and he *may* be allowed (or may not) to serve another church if he moves: and there is a priesthood which belongs inherently to all Christians, which a man may exercise when and where he is beyond the official, but not in opposition to, or in rivalry with, the official. That is what I meant.

APPENDIX 4

Letter to all Bishops attending 1930 Lambeth Conference

Amenbury,
Beaconsfield,
Bucks.
14th August, 1928.

My dear Bishop,
The subject of the little book which I am sending by this mail is, I am told, to be discussed at Lambeth in 1930, and I should like experience which I have gained at considerable pains to be at your disposal. The book is printed because I have been asked for more copies than I can supply without printing; and, since I have printed it, I am sending it to the members of the Lambeth Conference, in the hope that they may find something useful in it.

195

Our sons and friends overseas need something more than occasional Services provided _for_ them: they need the stimulus of personal activity; they need the fellowship of the Church and we know that mutural agreement to meet at the Holy Communion is the secret of that fellowship.

I have myself been almost surprised at the readiness of laymen to see what I mean, and to respond, when I have put the matter plainly to them. Small groups need full Church life. The supply of clergy to-day is quite inadequate for that, and consequently the task before us seems utterly beyond our powers.

We cannot but recognize that it is a rigid adherence to the stipendiary system which makes it impossible. A call for voluntary service would set us all free.

Believe me, My dear Bishop,

Yours sincerely,

Roland Allen.

Missionary Methods: St. Paul's or Satan's? an Infernal Dialogue

[This 'Socratic dialogue' was drafted whilst Roland was still living in Beaconsfield, probably in about 1930; but he did not even offer it to his traditional publishers, being convinced that they would think it either too flippant or too aggressive. Iohn suggested publication in the early 1940s: but then the idea was dropped, probably because the dialogue might well have seemed to be no more than a plagiarism of C. S. Lewis' similar idea in The Screwtape Letters, *published in 1942.]*

You remark how Plato describes Socrates standing at nightfall in the camp of the Greeks, lost in meditation, and how his fellow soldiers went to bed by the camp fires and lay watching him till they dropped off to sleep; and how in the morning when they woke they saw him still standing motionless just as he had been standing when they went to sleep. And how the sun rose, and then at last he moved, bowed himself down, and prayed, and went away.

I saw Satan standing just like that, and the leaders of the infernal hosts were watching him, just as the Greeks watched Socrates, only they were impatient and not merely curious; and at last Beelzebub could contain himself no longer:

Beelzebub: *What is the matter, Satan?* — he asked.

Satan: I was thinking about those Christian Missions.

B: *What about them? I have been away a long time: you know where. Nothing unusual has happened, has it? The Christians are still divided, aren't they? That was our trump suit. We always depended on that: internecine quarrels over Church doctrine and customs, words, and clothes, and ornaments and things like that, any number of them, something new every few years. They have not ceased, have they? You used to say that you were afraid that the vision of a world to be won for Christ would silence disputes and unite them. That hasn't happened, has it?*

S: No, it hasn't. Look at England today. The Church there is as excited about Tabernacles as if no one could be saved without them. Look at the world. The Christians, if they *were* united, would be only a small body in the midst of vast heathen populations; but they are not united. Those big-titled National Christian Councils do not matter. The separate missions go their own way in practice, and the Christians are all labelled *something* Christians: Roman Catholic Christians, Anglican Christians, Wesleyan Christians, Baptist Christians, and so on; and they more often drop the 'Christian' than the qualifying term, and are simply Roman Catholics, or Wesleyans, or Baptists, never simply Christians. They are scattered in these groups all over the countries, so that in many places, not only in whole provinces or in large towns, but even in little villages, there may be fragments of several groups. So there are dozens of organizations each providing for the welfare of its members scattered over wide areas, each doing the same or very much the same thing in the same places. That still holds up the procession.

B: *Well, you can always multiply divisions, can't you? You have never had much difficulty hitherto; and you have had plenty of experience. Twenty centuries have gone by and the Christians, taken all together, are still a comparatively small body in the world, and are divided as you say. Their missions will not do us much harm.*

S: I tell you they will. It is written: *'The earth shall be full of the knowledge of the Lord as the waters cover the sea'*. We cannot stop it, and these missions will assist it, and are assisting it.

B: *But we are hindering it, and we are fouling those waters.*

S: That is true. We are fouling them, sure enough. These people take their divisions abroad and the nations eat that which they have fouled with their feet and drink that which they have fouled with their feet: but still, it is time we did something.

B: *Wasn't it your idea to hand over the situation to Mammon? Didn't you put him in charge? What did he do about it?*

S: He did good work, very good work. He taught the zealots to put money in the first place.

B: *Money in the first place! They don't call that 'worshipping Mammon', do they?*

S: Of course not. They don't call it anything, they don't like to think about it; they just do it: we know what to call it. Mammon has always had individual Christians to worship him in plenty; but now he has fairly collared the machine.

B: *How did he do it?*

S: He *designed* the machine. You know what trouble we used to have with Christians. We had to be everywhere at once to keep an eye on them. The moment one left home on business, we never knew what might happen. A Church sprang up here, another there. And then evangelists went about wherever they liked, and we couldn't keep pace with them. Now in these days, if Christians acted like that, they go about in such numbers that we should never be able to keep in touch.

B: *Happily they don't. I am told that in religion as in everything*

199

else, these modern Western peoples have a strong caste feeling, and they do not like what they call inferior races to share their religion with them, if they have any. And the less they have, the less they like any of the other races to adopt a religion which is still nominally their own.

S: That is one of the facts on which Mammon relied. It seemed to them absolutely vain to imagine that the Christians would propagate the Gospel as the natural and inevitable effect of their scattering all over the world. No one even dreamed of attempting to arouse the Church, so that her children might do that.

B: *What else could they do?*

S: Look out for men who *did* understand the necessity for expansion, and *pay* them to to go.

B: *You mean, create a class of professional missionaries?*

S: Precisely. That is what Mammon did. He persuaded the people who were keen on extending the Church, or propagating the Gospel, or whatever they call it, to *begin* by collecting money and then paying professionals.

B: *Jolly for the pros! As long as they kept out of reach of their own people, life might be tolerable; but when the vast majority of the people who professed their religion either scoffed at them as fools, or refused to treat any converts as brethren, it must have made things difficult. It reminds me of the way in which we set those Judaizers in early years following Saul of Tarsus, and telling everybody he was a fraud.*

S: That was not such a big success as we thought it at the time. But at any rate they could not accuse Saul of Tarsus of being a pro. He took good care to avoid that. Mammon's great stroke consisted in creating a class of professionals, and putting the missionaries into it. Even if some had private means, and did not take any pay, Mammon got

200

them all into the same class, and built a wall of separation between that class and the ordinary Christians. That, and setting the people at home to believe that without money and professionals they would do nothing, was Mammon's great stroke.

B: *Then, I suppose, the well-disposed generally left everything to the pro. They would naturally do that.*

S: They generally did. All the bigwigs in the Church told them that it was their duty to support the professionals, and most of them satisfied their consciences by a subscription. And the people at home created great offices and organizations for collecting money, and issued appeal after appeal, and preached everywhere that nothing could be done without money.

B: *Did they get money?*

S: Mammon took a long view. He argued that the more they got, the more devoted they would be to money, and the more they would rely on it, and the more they would need it. And he was right.

B: *But if they got a lot of money, they would be able to support a host of evangelists.*

S: So they might have done, if I had not invented the Mission Station. But, even apart from that, they found it easier to get money than to get men. It is not everybody, who is really keen on propagating the Gospel, who wants to be a missionary pro. They never quite understood that, and they don't now. Of course you and I know that, to propagate a religion, *voluntary* service, which is obviously and unmistakably voluntary, is the strong weapon. No religion advances unless its adherents are keen to propagate it personally. We do not let our people employ many professionals to preach agnosticism or atheism, do we?

But an office, and an organization, and the collection of funds are wonderful things to blind the eyes. Still, I saw at once that there would be too many evangelists going about the world establishing Churches, unless we did something which would at once immobilize them, and use up large sums of money, and give them something *else* to establish. So I used the money to immobilize the men and, as I say, I invented the Mission Station, and let the establishment of mission stations take the place of establishing Churches. The professionals went out, and began buying land and houses, often in the face of local opposition which I encouraged. They built foreign churches and houses, and they established large institutions, all foreign of course. Whenever they made any converts, they settled down to look after them, and established these Stations. Then they wanted more money, and more, and more, and appealed perpetually to the people at home for it; and so the Societies never had enough. That had three great advantages: it bound the whole movement to the chariot wheels of Mammon, it misrepresented the purpose and work of the Christian missionaries, and it immobilized them and tied them up. I reckon that that one stroke put off the coming of Christ's kingdom for a millenium.

B: *I don't quite see that. Surely these mission stations were centres of light?*

S: You do not think that I was such a fool as to let it appear otherwise? Besides, I could not have helped it, if I had tried. All that I could do was to check them as far as possible. Do you think it was no gain to immobilize Christian missionaries, and especially Christian evangelists, and to get them well tied up in the business side of large stations? Do you think it was nothing to guide them gently into feeling more and more the need of money, and to start them on a road which meant no advance without *more* money? Do you think it was no advantage to make all the people round them suspicious of them, wondering what on earth they spent all that money on land and buildings for, and imagining all sorts of horrors, as that they were supported by their governments to get a footing in the country for political aggression? What do you think? Was all that nothing?

B: *I can see how it immobilized the sort of missionary who would enjoy running an institution, but you said it immobilized evangelists? I thought evangelists were essentially men who did not sit still. They did not in the early days. They were always on the move. If one of them stayed in a place two years, we used to think it a long time.*

S: The Evangelist—the real evangelist—is like that. He used to be always off creating a new Church somewhere. But you must remember that these men were agents of a Society which planted *stations*, not Churches. The difference between a Church and a mission station lies just here, that a Church can run itself, and a station cannot. The Station, when once established, must be looked after; and when the man in charge dies, or goes home, someone has to take charge, and if no one else is at hand they have to call in the evangelist and put *him* in charge, and the charge of a Station is no small work. It involves endless accounts and no end of petty business. A man is not free, when he has one of these Stations to look after. Consequently the evangelists—the *real* evangelists—often eat their hearts out running institutions and Stations. We cannot stop *all*: but you would be delighted to see how many we *do* stop, and how many we spoil. We immobilize the missionaries fairly well, considering. You have only to open up one of their own modern Surveys or Reports to see how many of the missionaries are tied up—four-fifths of them, or even nine-tenths of them, clustered in some two or three cities, or a few big stations. It's not bad.

203

B: *But you said that the mission stations misrepresented the Gospel of the missionaries, and made the people suspicious. How was that? Didn't the mission station bring immense advantages to the people? I thought they were the places where hospitals and schools and industrial workshops and all that sort of thing flourished?*

S: That is true. In dealing with things like Christian missions you cannot have it all your own way. All that you can do is to make as much mischief as possible. These mission stations involve the missionaries in worldly business; that is something: but in addition they do rouse suspicion. You can see for yourself. Suppose missionaries of a new Faith appear from a foreign land, and begin by buying land and houses, and settling down, don't you see that the people generally—especially if they have any reason to think that these foreigners are an aggressive race—must look at the proceeding with some suspicion? And if there is local opposition to begin with, and they overrule it, or get round it, either by offering a good price, or by appealing to treaty rights, or by insisting on their own governments support-ing them: isn't it quite obvious that the people will wonder what they are really aiming at? They may do a lot of charity, and win the hearts of many, but there will always be a large majority who will remain suspicious, and be-lieve that these foreigners are really playing the game of their own governments. They will say: 'Religion is not propagated in this way: the Buddhists did not propagate their religion like that, the Moslems do not: they taught the people what they believed, and men who were attracted by their teaching handed it on; but they did not come in and establish stations, like military outposts in other people's territory. There is more than religion behind all this.' That sort of suspicion dies hard. At intervals they butter up the missionaries who really do show charity and multiply good works; but the suspicion is always ready to break out into a flame at any provocation. To buy land and build houses and spend pots of money is such a strange way of propagating a religion that it is bound to create suspicion. And it has. Propagation of religion by the sword is intelligible; propagation by persuasion is intelligible; but this sort of thing is to most men quite *un*intelligible.

B: *But they don't think they can convert a nation by establishing these stations, do they? Why, they would need millions of money and hosts of men to do that!*

S: They are always saying that they do *not* expect to do that, but that is how they act. In spite of the obvious fact that their present stations are understaffed, and they are always crying out for more men and more money to maintain them, in spite of the fact that at intervals they have to close stations in order to spend more on great institutions, they still talk of any new advance as a matter of establishing a new Station.

B: *And do they not read the history of the early expansion of the Church? Those Christians, with whom we had to deal in early days, did not establish costly Stations, they established Churches; and a nice job we had with them.*

S: That is out of date today. Remember how we riddled those churches with heresies and schisms? *That* is what they read today, and they are afraid of it. I did not realize at the time what a victory we were winning. I didn't think that nineteen centuries later Christians would be dominated by the terror of it. Did you?

B: *But do they not preach Christ in these Stations?*

S: They do; but I took jolly good care they should preach something else as well.

B: *What?*

S: Oh, the old wheeze. 'The kingdom of God a kingdom to be

established by social advancement and intellectual enlightenment' and such like. Muddle up a lot of philanthropy in a bottle and label it 'Christian' and they will swallow it like . . . like gin. No—they wouldn't like that word: some of them are total abstainers or anti-alcoholists; we had better say 'like the sincere milk of the Word'. Anyway, they swallow it. And I have got missionaries, supported by these Societies, teaching the Chinese how to farm! Plenty of them are busy attacking social evils in detail. *That* keeps them busy.

B: *But didn't they make any converts?*

S: I couldn't help that. You know as well as I know that nothing stops Christ.

B: *Well, didn't those converts get on with the job, just as they used to do ages ago?*

S: I have learnt by experience, my friend! I didn't forget that lesson: you have forgotten Mammon, and his professionals.

B: *Did they make professionals of the converts?*

S: As many as they could. Enough to teach nearly all the converts to wait for the pro to act.

B: *Not all?*

S: No, not all. I tell you, I have had a difficult time. But still, the exceptions are comparatively rare.

B: *How did you manage it?*

S: They started, of course, as they had begun themselves. That was natural. They paid Christian workers to work for the Mission. That put off the lay Christian, who used to be our danger, wandering about and teaching others. Instead, he waited for the pro, or sent up a feeble bleat for one, because 'the propagation of the Gospel was not his

206

job'. But then I hammered it well in. The work was half done for me before I began, because these Western people have a natural tendency to worship what they call efficiency; and their efficiency is essentially something which can be measured in the scales of the world. They not only pay professionals to evangelize: they *train* them.

B: *What? Western people train Indians and Chinese to propagate the faith of Christ in their own land! You don't mean that, surely?*

S: I do. I mean just that. And, what is more, they set going the idea that men who have *not* been trained by them are not fit to propagate the Faith. They teach little boys in schools, and then catch as many of them as they can, and make them mission agents. In some schools they bind every boy who receives their money for his education under a contract to serve the mission as a teacher, or something of that kind, for a definite term of years.

B: *And they expect to get men to propagate a religion like that!*

S: They do. They are thoroughly convinced of it.

B: *But a few years' experience must teach them?*

S: Teach them what?

B: *That boys caught and trained like that cannot be efficient, if the propagation of the Gospel is what they want. You said they worship efficiency.*

S: Don't make any mistake here. You forget Christ. Some of these boys become really excellent and zealous evangelists and Christian teachers, because Christ lays hold of them.

B: *Yes, but the majority? Mere humdrum, uninspired, paid workers. They must find that out.*

S: They would, if they were not persuaded that, if the results are not what they would like, it is because the training has not been sufficiently thorough.

B: *So when things hang fire, they simply cry out for better training?*

S: That's it.

B: *Hooray! That puts the lid on it. A commercial mind applied to the propagation of a Faith! It's absolutely air-tight. The theory fits like the Gate of Hell: the more you try to escape, the closer you shut it; the more you open it, the less possible it is to pass out of it.*

S: Yes, that is so: but I am not easy in my mind. I saw a fellow once toiling and sweating at the Gate. I cheered him on. I said 'The only reason you fail lies in your lack of efficiency: you are strong enough; train harder; you have got hold of the right way to go to work: there's no doubt about that; just persevere.' I pointed out that the gate was actually opening. (You know that 'opening', which is really shutting). He went at it with all his might. And then, what do you think happened? Why, he suddenly turned round, and fled from it, crying: 'No hope'; and before you could wink he was *outside;* and the gate never opened at all, I swear it.

B: *Those gates never do open.*

S: Well, that is what I'm eternally afraid of with this Training Gate. It is all right at present. These missionaries are nearly all quite satisfied that all they need is more effort on their part, and greater efficiency in their training, and they think that the gate really is opening; but I have heard murmurings. I saw one man the other day scratching his head, and saying to himself: 'I wonder if this *is* the way?' And another went so far as to say: 'I wonder whether Christ does His *own* training?' I do not like it. That is what has set me musing.

B: *Cannot you keep them to the Training somehow? Why not try* *enlarging the idea of Training?*

S: I *have* done that, and I *am* doing it. At first their work was looked at as pure evangelism, and the missionaries were mocked and jeered at. Then they opened their educational establishments, and admitted more non-Christians than Christians, and gave them a Western education which fitted them for all sorts of useful jobs from the traders' and the governments' points of view; and they became more or less popular, and their work was applauded by statesmen. It was efficient, from their point of view. That tied up a very large number of missionaries, and caused the Societies to employ many who believed in scientific education above all things. They train not only Christian evangelists, but non-Christians for every kind of work. They think now of training not only the future leaders of the Church, but the leaders of the country generally. I think it fairly safe to say that they are spending more time and thought and money on this grandiose idea that they will lead whole nations than on their evangelistic work. The last catch-words are 'character training', and 'cooperation with governments' in the training of whole nations. That will mean, I hope and expect, that the Societies will become more and more absorbed in this kind of work. They will spend their energy and money on it; and in the event the governments will take charge and the education will be undisguisedly in their hands: and governments are religiously neutral, and are certainly not Christian missionary societies. That is all good, so far as it goes: but still I am not satisfied.

B: *Well, so far things seem to be going as well as you could expect. What was worrying you just now?*

S: I was trying to think how to put *another* spoke in their wheel.

B: *How?*

S: I want to exploit, for all it is worth, this new nationalist feeling.

B: *That seems simple enough. These missionaries hold all the positions of authority in their own hands, don't they?*

S: They ordain a certain few natives of the country after a long and careful training in their *own* way of doing things, and at rare intervals a Bishop, and they admit natives to councils, so long as there appears to be no danger of their doing anything but run the machine in the usual way. And the Christians everywhere depend very largely (thanks to Mammon) on supplies of money from abroad, and are always fearful lest the supplies may be cut off. Hitherto Mammon has urged that the money ought to be the bone of contention, and that I ought to encourage the native Christian leaders to seek after and covet the positions and stipends of the missionaries. He argued that the refusal of the missionaries to give up those positions and stipends to the natives, on the grounds that they were not sufficiently well trained, would cause a deep and growing discontent on the side of the native Christians of ability. I cannot deny that it is working well. The young Christian leaders trained in the missionary colleges are getting restive, and demanding the first places. Their minds are set on the positions and the stipends, and there is a good hope that they will make trouble before long. Money and position are without doubt splendid bones of contention. I do not want to drop that policy. But I want, if I can, to introduce another element of discord. If only the young native leaders were to see that money and position is of small importance compared with *spiritual* authority, they would accuse the missionaries of holding all spiritual authority in their own hands, and of dominating over them spiritually; and that would mean a first class row, and probably in the event a huge schism, on racial lines.

210

B: *But most of these missionaries declare that they do not believe in any spiritual authority which they can give, or retain.*

S: That is all very fine. They talk like that. But indeed they *act* as if they had spiritual authority over their converts. They teach their own doctrine and their forms of worship and their Christian customs, and they generally dictate the terms on which converts are to be received; and they run their stations just as those who talk openly about having spiritual authority. The natives do not see much difference.

B: *Well then, the position and the salary involve the authority. If the native Christians fight for the position and salary, in effect they will be fighting for the authority.*

S: No, it is not quite the same thing. Outside some Protestant denominations all men know that an organized society must have officers with authority; and that officers in a spiritual society must have spiritual authority. Now, so long as they simply grumble because the foreigners retain positions which they covet, they think of the authority as a kind of social authority, just as men think of positions under the government: but if they come to think of spiritual authority in a spiritual society as a gift held by men who received it to hand it on; then all their highest and best instincts will be roused to furious indignation. I tell you, it makes a lot of difference whether they think of positions simply as positions of dignity and emoluments, or whether they think of spiritual power withheld.

B: *But you do not want them to have spiritual power? If they had it, they might escape out of that network of mission station control, which you have been saying has done our work so well, and has restricted the propagation of the Gospel so narrowly.*

S: I do not want them to *have* it; but I do want them to fight for it: for, as I said, no other conceivable cause of strife and division would drive them so mad.

B: *You cannot do it. The missionaries might give way.*

S: Not for a long time. They are mightily afraid for their doctrine and their customs, and they are persuaded that any spiritual freedom of their converts would mean the destruction of both. Didn't you hear that man the other day arguing that missionaries must *control*? He was saying what nine-tenths of the missionaries think. They would not easily hand over spiritual authority, and they would use the power of the purse (again thanks to Mammon) to retain it, in fact, if not in appearance, in their own hands.

B: *But if these native Christians once saw what spiritual authority and freedom meant, they would not care a rap about the money.*

S: Of course they would not; but they will be divided. A few may see the spiritual authority, the majority will seek the material and social position all the time. What I want is to give that majority who are really seeking the stipends and position the support of a few men who really see the spiritual authority, and give them all a cry which will upset the foreign missionaries, and add that sting to their attack which is only found where spiritual issues are thought to be at stake. With one voice they will all cry: 'You retain all spiritual authority in your own hands, and strive to be Lords over God's heritage!'. That is a far better cry than 'You retain positions and stipends which we covet!'

B: *But the missionaries will foresee that, and—as they sincerely believe that they do not want to withhold anything that is good for their converts—they will hasten to give way.*

S: You are wrong on both points: the missionaries will *not* foresee it. They foresee nothing until it happens. They had very good reasons for foreseeing that the Chinese would resent their establishment of mission colleges in China: but when the Chinese Educational Associations passed resolutions demanding their registration under the Government, they were taken by surprise. And they may not want to withhold anything that is good, but they will withhold *this*, because they will not believe that the native Christians are sufficiently well trained to use it wisely. Did you never hear that playful answer to a child: 'Those who ask won't get; those who don't ask don't want'? If the natives are humble and wait, they may wait; if they ask, they show that they have not the humility which is the first virtue of men who hold spiritual power.

B: *But someone will point out to them that they are in danger of a serious setback to their highest hopes.*

S: Let him. If an angel from heaven told them what we have been saying, they would not believe him. They would accuse him of being an opponent of foreign missions, and an uncharitable and wicked critic of better men than himself. I am not afraid of that.

B: *Satan, I fear that you will overreach yourself. Mammon, you said, did well: yet just think of the prayerful giving by multitudes of pious people; think of the lives laid down. That is all terrible. That spirit of devotion and self-sacrificing charity will prevail. One day it will be made manifest, and it will work wonders, in spite of all that Mammon can do, or you either, for all your cunning. And here again you will fail. You may make trouble, but you will fail.*

S: No doubt I shall fail: we are fated to fail. If we can make trouble anywhere, and use the best spiritual aspirations of men to make trouble, that is all we can hope to do. And I can do it here. I will set these native Christians crying: 'You deny us that spiritual authority which alone can enable us to do our proper work as Christians'.

B: *If you do that, you will run an awful risk. Spiritual authority is a spiritual thing, and if they seek it, they will get it. It is not*

213

simply a question here of a thing like a salary. Take my advice, and do not stir men up to seek spiritual gifts.

S: I tell you, it is the only way. If I did not make it a bone of contention, if the authority were given freely, you know what would happen. If the Christians in China, or in India, or in Africa were really a *native* Church, endowed with spiritual authority which not only native Christians but *white men* must recognise, then we should be at our wits' end, progress would be so rapid. The only way to prevent that is to make spiritual authority a subject of dispute. That will at least produce a first-class schism, bigger than any that we have yet seen.

B: *You will overreach yourself. I am certain of it. Schisms do not last for ever.*

S: They last long; and they do no end of harm to the cause of Christ.

B: *I give it up. I see that all things are in train for this. The hour for its coming is not far off. You were working while you were meditating all that long time. It will come; but it will work out very differently from your calculations.*

S: Bunkum! In the long run, yes, I am bound to lose; but for this age I win.

—————

Roland Allen
Amenbury
Beaconsfield
Bucks.

transcribed by Hubert Allen, with some expanded abbreviations and added punctuation, from the much corrected manuscript in Rhodes House, Oxford: March 1994

214

Letter withdrawing assistance from St. Mark's Church, Nairobi

TO THE COMMUNICANTS AT ST. MARK'S CHURCH.

Nov. 26. 1939

Since Mr. Harper left, I have been invited by Mr. Johnes to take a service at St. Mark's from time to time. I have now taken many, and I feel a considerable interest in the welfare of St. Mark's, though I have never had any opportunity of meeting the Church Committee.

Now I want the Communicants at St. Mark's to consider their action seriously, and to understand mine.

There are not enough stipendiary clergy to supply all the congregations. In seeking to secure one of them you are thinking only of yourselves. You are looking only on your own things, not on the things of others. That is *selfish*; it is not a right attitude for Christian men.

Your experience in the past should have taught you that it is not a wise action. You cannot be sure that the stipendiary who comes to you is the right man, or his wife, if he has one, the right woman, to assist the life of the Church. Nor can you be sure that he will stay long. You are always in danger of being left again.

The only way to avoid these evils is to provide clergy from among those settled here, men already known to you as sound men, regular worshippers at St. Mark's, men who really do lead you in the right way and can sympathize with you in your temptations, knowing by experience the conditions in which you live. That would not be selfish; for it would show the way in which every other congregation of Christians in the world might have full Church life. It would be an expression of real charity . . .

A Church ought to be a properly organized Body with its own leaders and ministers. The idea that all that is necessary is to find some cleric, who happens to be at liberty or desires a change, to hold services is an utterly false conception. When no such cleric can be found, the rites of the Church cease, and it is at once apparent that the Church, so called, is, not a Church, but a parasite.

To turn now to my action. Hitherto I have been asked simply to fill gaps. I cannot continue to do that. It is not right. Gaps are an inevitable part of the present system, and those who accept the system must accept the gaps as part of it. It is no true kindness to make an evil more tolerable, when the evil ought to be removed. If I see a man wallowing in a miry slough it is my duty, not to make his position in it a little less painful and by doing so to help him imagine that the slough is not very bad, but to convince him, if I can, that his position is very bad, and that he must get out of it. I would gladly serve St. Mark's if my service helped you out of the mire; but I cannot serve, if my service helps you to remain in it.

With all my heart I wish you well. I warn you that action taken solely to secure what you think to be to your own advantage, regardless of others, is not the way to gain the blessing of God, and it is God's blessing that I desire for you. I am,

Yours very sincerely,
(Signed) *Roland Allen*

216

References[1]

Books, Articles[2] and Pamphlets by Roland Allen

The Case for Voluntary Clergy. London: Eyre & Spottiswoode, 1930.

'The Case for Voluntary Clergy: an Anglican Problem'. *The Interpreter* (July 1922), pp. 314ff.

'The Church and an Itinerant Ministry.' *The East & the West*, 25/98 (April 1927), pp.123-133.

Devolution and its Real Significance. With A. Mcleish. World Dominion Press, 1927.

Educational Principles & Missionary Methods. London: Robert Scott, 1919. (In the Library of Historic Theology.)

'The Establishment of Indigenous Churches.' Unpublished. 1927.

Foundation Principles of Foreign Missions. Privately printed by Richard Clay & Sons, Bungay, Suffolk, circa 1910.

'The Influence of Foreign Missions on the Church at Home'. *The Commonwealth*, XVIII/212 (December 1913), pp. 382-396.

'Islam and Christianity in the Sudan'. *International Review of Missions*, IX/36 (October 1920), pp. 531-543.

'Letter to the Parishioners of Chalfont St Peter', November 25th, 1907. Reprinted in *The Ministry of the Spirit*, pp. 193-197.

'The Ministry of Expansion: the Priesthood of the Laity.' Unpublished. 1930.

---

[1] This list of references does not, of course, attempt to provide a full bibliography, for which the reader is referred to e.g. Paton, *The Ministry of the Spirit*; Sanderson, *Roland Allen and his Vision*; or Talltorp, *Sacrament & Growth*.

[2] Numerous articles in *The Land of Sinim* and *World Dominion* are also cited; these and others, and newspaper articles and letters, are listed in e.g. Sanderson.

Missionary Methods: St. Paul's or Ours? A Study of the Church in the Four Provinces. London: Robert Scott:, February 1912 (in the Library of Historic Theology); reprinted October 1913. Revised edition published by World Dominion Press, August 1927; reprints 1930, 1949, 1956. Reset—with memoir by Alexander McLeish—Wm.B.Eerdmans Publishing Co: Grand Rapids, Michigan, 1962; reprint 1993.

Missionary Principles. Robert Scott, 1913; [also published in New York—title: *Essential Missionary Principles*] Reprinted 1964 by Lutterworth Press.

Missionary Survey as an Aid to Intelligent Cooperation in Foreign Missions. With Thomas Cochrane. World Dominion Press, 1920.

'Money the Foundation of the Church'. *The Pilgrim*, 6/4 (July 1926), pp. 417-428.

'The "Nevius Method" in Korea'. *World Dominion*, July 1930, pp. 252-258.

Non-Professional Missionaries. Amenbury, 1929.

'Of some of the Causes which led to the Preservation of the Foreign Legations in Peking.' *Cornhill Magazine*, No. 492 (December 1900).

'Of some of the Causes which led to the Siege of the Foreign Legations at Peking.' *Cornhill Magazine,* No. 491 (November 1900).

'Of some of the Conclusions which may be drawn from the Siege of the Foreign Legations in Peking.' *Cornhill Magazine*, No. 494 (February 1901).

Pentecost & the World: the Revelation of the Holy Spirit in the Acts of the Apostles. London; Oxford University Press, 1917; [reprinted (shorn of its preface and detailed analysis of its contents) in *The Ministry of the Spirit*, pp. 1-61].

'The Priesthood of the Church'. Church Quarterly Review (Jan. 1933) pp. 233-244.

Sidney James Wells Clark—a Vision of Foreign Missions. World Dominion Press, 1937.

The Siege of the Peking Legations. London: Smith Elder & Co., 1901.

The Spontaneous Expansion of the Church, and the Causes which Hinder It. World Dominion Press, 1927; reprinted 1949, 1956; new edition 1962.

Translations from the Swahili:

    'Inkishafi'. African Studies, December 1946.

    'The Story of Mbega' [part 1] by Abdullah bin Hemedi 'lAjjemy. *Tanganyika Notes & Records,* 1936-1937.

    'Utenzi wa Abdirrahmani na Sufiyani' by Hemed Abdalla el Buhry. *Johari za Kiswahili,* No. 2 (1961).

    'Utenzi wa Kiyama (Siku ya Hukumu)'. Supplement to *Tanganyika Notes & Records,* circa 1946.

    'Utenzi wa Kutawafu Naby' (author unknown). Supplement to *Journal of the East African Swahili Committee,* June 1956. [Re-edited as 'Utendi wa Kutawafu Nabii', Edward Mellen Press, 1991.]

Voluntary Clergy Overseas—an Answer to the Fifth World Call. Amenbury, 1928.

Voluntary Clergy. SPCK, 1923.

La Zoute—a Critical Review of 'The Christian Mission in Africa'. World Dominion Press, 1927.

Collections of writings by Roland Allen:

Paton, D.M., ed. *The Ministry of the Spirit.* World Dominion Press, 1960.

——— *Reform of the Ministry.* Lutterworth Press, London, 1968.

—————— and Charles L. Long, eds. *The Compulsion of the Spirit: a Roland Allen Reader.* Wm.B.Eerdmans/Forward Movement, 1983.

Books and Articles by other Authors

Allen, I.W.T. 'Muslims in East Africa'. *African Ecclesiastical Review,* July 1965.

Allen, Priscilla M. 'Roland Allen — a Prophet for this Age'. *The Living Church,* 192/16 (April 20, 1986).

Allen, R. M. 'Notes for a Life of Willoughby Charles Allen.' c.1975.

Barry, F. R. *The Relevance of the Church.* Nisbet, 1935.

Beyerhaus, P. and H. Lefever. *The Responsible Church & the Foreign Mission.* World Dominion Press, 1964.

Boer, Harry R. 'Roland Allen, the Holy Spirit, and Missions'. *World Dominion,* XXXIII/5, (September-October, 1955).

—————— *Pentecost & Missions.* Grand Rapids: Wm. B. Eerdmans, 1961.

Brammer, John E. Brammer. 'Roland Allen: Pioneer in a Spirit-Centred Theology of Mission'. *Missiology,* V/2 (April 1977).

Carter, David J. 'The Archbishop's Western Canada Fund & the Railway Mission'. *Saskatchewan History,* XXII/1 (Winter 1969).

—————— 'The Railway Mission–Regina'. *Journal of Canadian Church Historical Society,* X/4 (December 1968).

Cochrane Thomas. *Atlas of China in Provinces showing Missionary Occupation.* Christian Literature Society for China, 1913.

—————— *Survey of the Missionary Occupation of China.* Christian Literature Society for China, 1913.

Davis, Gerald C., ed. *Setting Free the Ministry of the People of God.* Cincinnati: Forward Movement Publications, 1984.

REFERENCES

Denniston, R.A. *Part-Time Priests—a Discussion*. Skeffington & Sons, 1960.

Donovan, Vincent J. sj. Christianity *Rediscovered: an Epistle from the Masai*. SCM Press, 1978.

French, Francesca. *Thomas Cochrane: Pioneer & Missionary Statesman*. Hodder & Stoughton, 1956.

Fuller, J. and P. Vaughan. *Working for the Kingdom: the Story of Ministers in Secular Employment*. SPCK, 1986.

Grubb, Sir Kenneth. 'The Story of the Survey Application Trust'. [in Paton, *Reform of the Ministry*].

Hargrave, Alan. *But who will preside?* Nottingham: Grove Books, 1990.

Jackson-Brown, Irene. *Ministry Development Journal*, No.15 (1988). 18 items on application of RA's principles.

Kelley, H.H., ssm. 'Ministry & the Church: their Relations'. *The Review of the Churches*, VI/3, (July 1929).

King, Noel Q. 'Last Years in East Africa'. [In *Reform of the Ministry*].

Long, Charles H. & Anne Rowthorn. 'The Legacy of Roland Allen'. *International Bulletin of Missionary Research*, April 1989.

McGavran, Donald A. *The Bridges of God: a Study in the Strategy of Missions*. World Dominion Press, 1955.

McLeish, Alexander. 'Biographical Memoir'. [in Paton, ed., *The Ministry of the Spirit*.]

Metzner, Hans Wolfgang. *Roland Allen: sein Leben und Werk*. Gütersloh: Gütersloher Verlagshaus Gerd Mohn, 1970.

Neill, Stephen Neill. *Colonialism & Christian Missions*. Lutterworth, 1966.

Nevius, John L. *Methods of Mission Work*. China Inland Mission, 1898.

221

Norris, Frank L. *China*. No.3 in Mowbray's series of Handbooks of English Church Expansion, 1908.

Paton, D.M., ed. *New Forms of Ministry*. Research Pamphlet No.12, Edinburgh House Press, 1965.

Ransome, Jessie. *The Story of the Siege Hospital in Peking*. London: SPCK, 1901.

Renouf, Robert W. 'Anglicanism in Nicaragua 1745-1985'. *Anglican & Episcopal History*, 57/4, (December 1988).

Sanderson, David. 'Roland Allen: a Prophet for a "Decade of Evangelism"'. *Quarterly of the Modern Churchpeople's Union*, XXXIV/4 (1993).

Sanderson, David. *Roland Allen and his Vision of the Spontaneous Expansion of the Church*. Lambeth Diploma thesis, 1989.

Society for the Propagation of the Gospel. *Report of the Bicentenary*. 1901.

Talltorp, Åke. *Sacrament & Growth: a Study in the Sacramental Dimension of Expansion in the Life of the Local Church, as reflected in the Theology of Roland Allen*. Uppsala, Sweden: 1989.

Williams, W.R. *Ohio Friends in the Land of Sinim*. Mount Gilead, Ohio: 1925.

Index

Alfred, Prince [Duke of Edinburg] 63–64
Ali Hemedi el Buhriy 163
Allen, Arthur 15, 178
Allen, Beatrice Mary (née Tarleton) ix–x, 63, 67, 170, 178
Allen, Catherine (née Brown) 178
Allen, Catherine Ellen (née Green) 165, 178
Allen, Charles Fletcher 10, 178
Allen, Derick 84
Allen, Ellen Ida ('Nellie') 15, 178
Allen, Frederick W. x
Allen, Iohn ix, 77, 101, 112, 152–153, 162, 178, 180–181
Allen, James Roger 10, 178
Allen, John 10, 178
Allen, Lionel Raymond 9
Allen, Priscilla ix, 70, 81, 87, 101, 111–112, 154, 178, 180
Allen, Priscilla [née Malpas] 9, 11, 12, 178
Allen, Reginald 15, 178
Allen, Richard M. x, 84
Allen, Roland
  ancestry 9–10, 178
  as linguist 27, 100, 161
  as teacher 30, 114
  death 169
  debater 17, 30
  education 15
  engagement 65
  health 18, 115–116
  honeymoon 69
  memory 95
  ordination 20
  preacher 100

sense of humor   145
views
  on laity   81
  on money   82
  on polygamy   173
wedding   67, 69
Allen, Willoughby Charles   x, 16–17, 69, 109, 178
Allen, Winifred E. E. [née Brooke]   ix, 84, 114, 154, 178
Altar of Heaven   24
Amenbury (Beaconsfield)   109, 117
American Board Mission (Peking)   27
Anglican Mission (Peking)   27
Archbishops' Western Canada Fund   130
Assam (India)   viii–ix, 119, 133, 137
Azariah, Vedanayakam Samuel   86, 129, 137, 152

Barry, F.R.   144
Bath College   17
Beaconsfield (Buckinghamshire)   109
Belize (British Honduras)   10
Bewes, Peter   122
Birt, R.H.C.   136
Boer, Harry R.   103, 106
Boff, Leonardo   xiv
Book of Common Prayer   4
Boxer movement   37, 44, 58
Brandreth, Edith Finetta (née Tarleton)   64, 78, 85, 178
Brightman, F.E.   69
Brightman, Frank Edward   19
Bristol Grammar School   17
British Honduras   10
Burford (Oxfordshire)   69

Capablanca, José   168
Chakrabarti, Rev'd.   149

Chalfont St. Peter (Buckinghamshire) 75, 77, 183
Chamberlain, Finetta (née Brandreth) x, 84
Chesterton, G.K. 110
Ch'i-Chou (China) 73
Clark, Sidney J.W. viii, 2, 90, 91, 109, 115
Clissold, Hannah 11, 12
Cochrane, Thomas 91, 117
Cockburn, H. 48
Crickhowell (Wales) 69

Darlington (Durham) 20
Derby (England) 10
Dimsdale, Thomas 68
Donovan, Vincent xiv
Dornakal (India) 137

East Africa 154
Ecumenical Movement 6
Educational Principles & Missionary Methods 101
Exeter College 16

Fifth World Call 124
Fliess, Hermann 167
Fliess, Ralph 167
Fliess, Valerie x, 167
Foundation Principles of Foreign Missions 85

Gairdner, William Henry Temple 85, 120
Gielgud, John 101
Glover, T.R. 17
Goldstein, Dr. 168
Gore, Charles 19, 88, 102
Grubb, Sir Kenneth 90, 92, 159
Gwynne, Llewellyn 142, 152

Han-ko-Chuang (China)   72
Harnack, Adolf von   85
Harpenden (Hertfordshire)   83, 99
Holmes, Martin R.   x
Holmes, Sir Charles   16, 110
Hubback, George Clay   137, 148
Hung, Miss   44
Hutton, W.H.   18

India   86, 119, 129, 133
indigenous principles   118

Jessie Ransome   62
Jones, Catherine Mary ['Katie' née Allen]   15, 178
Junkison, Frederick   136

Kelly, Herbert Hamilton   110, 123
Kennedy, Dr. and Mrs.   86
Kenya   119, 154
Ketteler, Baron von   48
Knowles, Archdeacon   131

Lambert, Miss   39, 47
The Land of Sinim   28
Lei Yü Ch'ün   42, 72
Lewis, Clive Staples   159
Lloyd, Edgar   133
Lu Kou Ch'iao (China)   38

Madagascar Revisited   92
Malpas, Catherine Emma   12
Malpas, Henry   178
Malpas, Joseph Henry   12, 178

Maurice, F.D.   107
McLeish, Alexander   115
Milford, Humphrey   124
The Ministry of Expansion: the Priesthood of the L   160
The Ministry of the Spirit   106, 120, 146
Missionary Methods—St. Paul's or Ours?   92, 175
Missionary Methods: St. Paul's or Ours?   86
Missionary Principles   88
Murray, Gilbert   110
Murray, Lady Mary   110

Nagasaki (Japan)   58
Nairobi (Kenya)   154, 215
Nash, J.O.   136
Neill, Stephen   103
Newbigin, Lesslie   vii, 121, 171
Ningpo (China)   31
Niu-Chang (China)   31
Non-Professional Missionaries   120
Norman, H.V.   28, 73
Norris, Frank L.   41, 44, 55, 70
North China Mission   22, 56, 74, 78
North China Mission Association   56, 62, 64

Oxford
   St. John's College   18
Oxford Mission to Calcutta   138
Oxford University
   Ramsden Sermon   100

Paddock, Robert   130
Paton, David   viii
Paul the Apostle, Saint   102, 174
Peking (China)   22–32, 71
Peking [Beijing] (China)   36

Pentecost & the World   105–106, 146, 175
Pentecost and the World   104
Pilling, John K.   x
Plymouth Brethren   12
Porter, H. Boone   x
Pretoria (South Africa)   101, 133
Primrose Hill (London)   83
Pusey House   xiv, 18

Ramsay, William Mitchell   17, 85
Ransome, Edith   39, 46
Ransome, Jessie   39, 46, 69, 70
Reform of the Ministry   160
Reid, Dr. Gilbert   40
Rhodes House (Oxford)   x
Rhodesia   119, 133
Ripon Cathedral   101
Rohilla (H.M.S.)   91, 94
Roman Catholic Church   27
Rumuruti (Kenya)   157
Rusapi (Rhodesia)   133

S.J.W. Clark: a Vision of Missions   158
Saben, Mrs. Barbara   x
Saham Toney (Norfolk)   154
Sanderson, David   x
Scott, Charles Perry   22, 39, 69
Scott, Mrs. Francis   39, 58
The Screwtape Letters   159, 197
Seth-Smith, David   110, 113
Shanghai (China)   34
Shantung (China)   27, 32, 41
Shih Hung Chang   41, 72
Shih Min Chuang (China)   72
The Siege of the Peking Legations   iii

Smuts, Jan Christiaan   89
South Africa   119, 133
Southern Rhodesia   156
The Spontaneous Expansion of the Church   94, 107, 129
Stelle, W.B.   37
Sudan   152
Survey Application Trust   xiv, 108, 115

Talltorp, Åke   x, 127
T'ang (writer)   49
Tanga (Tanganyika)   154
Tarleton, Alfred Henry   62, 63, 94, 109, 178
Tarleton, Finetta (née Dimsdale)   178
Tarleton, Mary Beatrice   62
Tarleton, Sir (John) Walter   62–64, 178
Tarleton, Sir Banastre   68
Temple of Heaven   56
Tientsin (China)   22, 57
T'ung-Chou (China)   57

Umtata (Rhodesia)   133
[United] Society for the Propatgation of the
      Gospe   x, 22, 56, 59

Victoria, Queen   62–63
Voces populi de parabolis Christi   159
Voluntary Clergy   130
voluntary clergy   4–5
Voluntary Clergy Overseas   124, 143, 145

Waggett, Philip   19, 88
Wang-Shu-T'ien   31, 42, 72
Warren, Mrs. C.P.S.   109
Wei-Hai-Wei (China)   31
Westcott, Brooke Foss   20

Whitehead, Henry   86, 144
Williams, Charles   124
Willingen (Germany)   vii
World Council of Churches   vii
World Missionary Conference (1910)   85
Wynn-Williams, Mary   84
Wynn-Williams, Watkin   84

YMCA, Rouen (France)   99
Yung-Ch'ing (China)   41, 70–71, 72